The Kidnapping of Ginger

A DHS Atrocity

Gary DeCarlo

G & G Publishing

Acknowledgments

Without the monetary gift from my dad, my quest to retrieve my daughter would have been at best greatly compromised. As he knows, I will forever be grateful for his love and life and what it allowed me to do. It has touched more lives as a result than my dad could ever fathom.

I would like to thank Sone for her support of this book. Having someone to listen, suggest, and be in tune with points I tried conveying was essential.

Thank you, Attorney Cory McClure, who took my case when he didn't have to, and gave me hope when I felt there was none.

Table of Contents

Preface

THE UNTAINTED LOVE for my girl was matched in horror when she was stolen. With each passing day, week, and month, the gravity of the situation escalated. I resigned from my job and spent one year fighting a daunting battle with the state, DHS, and Family Court. With little knowledge I was ambushed by everybody and everything I came across. As a single father without my name on the birth certificate, allegations I abused my girlfriend, and the case in dreaded Family Court, I was ridiculed, humiliated, and dismissed at every turn. Only my love for my innocent daughter Ginger, propelled me to fight every day at any cost. I researched similar cases and found an epidemic of states snatching children without cause. The broad language, "The best interest of the child," is used at the state's convenience. With Ginger's seizure, the state's criteria of "imminent danger or neglect" was blatantly disregarded. Once DHS steps in, major trouble arrives. Anonymous tips lead to knocks on your door without verification of those tips. Children are taken while parents, most with limited resources, are at the mercy of CPS, DHS, Juvenile Court, and state employees. And they are all linked. One agency feeds the other. Do not trust any of them. Get counsel immediately. Watch anything you say. Record anything you can. Do not let anyone in your house without a warrant. Reserve your cooperation. Once those institutions are involved in your life, the way you knew life is over. You will be required to take a substance-abuse evaluation and most likely treatment, a mental-health assessment (with therapy, recommended or not), parenting classes (some six weeks), and random drug tests. Trying to maintain a job through this involvement will be most likely impossible.

I was living the horror stories I read. I knew what others were feeling. Story after story chronicled abuse of power. There was one common denominator: nobody governs these state agencies; consequently abuse goes unpunished. With nothing to deter the abuse, the empowerment escalates out of control. Combining those with power and little accountability leads to abuse at every level. An example is law enforcement. Why are mini cams required in most jurisdictions? Abuse of power. Empower anyone with little transparency, and abuse is inevitable. How many riots happened as a result? We should hope body cams may change some of that. The same is happening with Social Services. They are stealing children. A national disgrace. I don't condone violence, but civil unrest is in order. With CPS and DHS there cannot be immunity. Immunity parallels no accountability. The system is beyond broke. It's crushed. Well-meaning parents suffering the most emotional trauma imaginable. Kids are taken in the middle of the night with no recourse. Families are shredded like lettuce under the guise of "Best interest of the Child" rhetoric. It's criminal. Kids are taken by states every day and every hour across the country. Their motive to take children and move them to foster care? Federal funding and workers' own job security.

My objective in writing this book is to show it's real for those being investigated, victimized, and lied to, with no forum to be heard. It all happened to me. If it can happen to a retired white former teacher in suburbia, it can happen to anyone, anywhere at any time. A knock on the door from DHS may come from an anonymous tip, a person with a vendetta, or a neighbor across the street. A phone call is all it takes. "Choose your battles wisely" never made more sense. When I told friends of my case, time and again they would say, "Write a book." Only after reading the accounts of others, while enduring heartache I sustained, did I decide to write one. Not as much for a shot at reform, but a way to help at least one family, navigate the broken system better than I.

I have chronicled the actual events, dates, dialogue, and happenings as they unfolded. Some sections and chapters were written the day they occurred. I have italicized my attitudes and thoughts in the body to describe my mindset, for good or bad, as they occurred over one horrific year. The characters are real. Their names, dialogue, and attitudes are equally real. And lastly, this narrative is spotted with dry, and at times self-enhanced humor. Without it I would not have been able to complete my task. It was my only salvation and vindication, the only way to express my contempt for both the system and the participating characters. I make no apologies to anyone I may have offended.

The Names Have Not been Changed to Protect the Guilty.

Introduction

IF YOU ARE reading this, Princess, then I am gone. But please don't cry. Embrace instead. My intent is to provide thought, pleasure, and comfort. Two days before your first birthday thoughts of writing you a time capsule monopolized my day. Almost a year to the day the uncertainty I felt when God delivered our "gift" was overwhelming, and for one reason only: my age of fifty-six. The uncertainty vanished the moment I saw you. The upside of my age is I cherished every moment with you.

(An excerpt I wrote on Ginger's first birthday titled *Time Capsule*. It contains anecdotes, advice, encouragement, and love. The intent is to give to her after my death or when appropriate.)

First seeing Ginger Rae is like stepping outside into bright light. With perfect brows sculpted, eyes blue as the sky, she comes with a spirit that is undeniable. Not yet four, she is the centerpiece of our home, tucked away, in perhaps the quietest neighborhood in Des Moines. But nobody is as happy as we think we should be. Selfish? Perhaps. Entitlement? Most likely. Every day aspires to be different from the last. Attitude is vital. Without a good attitude we find the house, my job, and Ginger's demands unbearable. It carries harshly into our once-quiet intimate world. I'm constantly reflecting on what I can do to keep Ginger on task. Must be my age, I ponder. I'm not physically what I was. Far from it. It's what I hoped wouldn't happen.

Internally I blame work demands. I blame Nicole, my partner of seven years and twenty years my junior. We hope to find a groove, an understanding to smooth this not-so-smooth ride. Stress has reared its head, and that is not a good thing.

I have preached before and after her birth that calm parents have calm children. This message has fallen onto completely deaf ears. I don't recall it being remotely like this. Is it me? Of course I share in what appears to be everyday chaos.

But wait. It's not me. Fast forward to January 11, 2019. A deplorable breach by the state's DHS and the thrashing of our civil rights paralyzed everyone without knowing for how long. I see why there was daily chaos, a polluted household, severe mood swings, and secrets upon secrets. DHS has abducted my Ginger.

CHAPTER One

Secrets on Secrets

3/10/2017
Des Moines, Iowa

IT STARTED WITH Tiffanie, Nicole's other daughter, all of fourteen, biracial, and running wild. The sex and drugs would not wait. When she was a freshman at Hoover High School, a half mile from our home, the signs of problems started quickly and succinctly. She never went a week without missing one or two days. Nicole, her mother and my partner of seven years did try, extremely hard, but there was no controlling her. She would look at us and smile and politely lie her ass off. There was just one way to control her: chain her up, but that was illegal.

The lessons I wrote in *Time Capsule* for Ginger to use as a reference some day, were the same lessons I preached to Tiffanie. Not only were they ignored, I suspect they were scoffed at. That is fine I thought; it's you who will pay the consequences. But little did I know the consequences would be paid by everyone—severe consequences by the guilty, the not-so-guilty, and tragically, the completely innocent, Ginger.

Tiffanie's delinquent behavior soon led to pregnancy by a twenty-year-old wretch charged with statutory rape. Prison soon followed for Austin Bell. But along with it came DHS rearing its ungoverned head. With the pregnancy Nicole, Tiffanie, and I sat down to discuss her options. Open adoption offered the best of both worlds, I explained. You have periodic access to your child. You build and maintain a bond. This while you grow up, finish school, and figure out the direction of your life. Sounds reasonable, they said. But everything sounded reasonable. In this house listening and adhering were two different things. Prior to this they considered abortion, but after procrastinating, I was told it was too late to abort. Just like kids having kids, Tiffanie gave birth to a daughter. DHS, having been told, I said, "If you have that child, I'm throwing you out," made arrangements for her at Harbour, a home for teenage moms. This would be the first in a litany, of unscrupulous lies about me.

4/1/2018
(One year later)

I HAD BEEN working full time at Goodwill Industries as a clerk for one year, allowing Nicole to stay home full time with Ginger. Prior to this job I was a substitute school teacher on and off for twenty years. In between teaching I worked at three major organizations: Midamerican Energy, Boys & Girls Clubs of Central Iowa, and Prairie Meadows Casino. Nearing sixty, I was ready to retire, hang out, and help raise my little girl.

As I come up the stairs ready for work, two properly dressed woman with probing eyes are speaking to Nicole in the living room. Here again, I thought, thinking it odd, as Tiffanie had long been sent to Harbour. Later that night I asked Nicole why DHS was still coming here, and for the second or third time was told it was some sort of follow-up meeting. I will regret my naivete and trust till the day I die. *I knew it wasn't about Tiffanie.*

It felt like DHS, when questioning Nicole about Tiffanie, spotted this gorgeous blue-eyed four-year-old, my Ginger, and decided she was now our focal point. It's obvious there was no imminent danger or neglect to this happy, inquisitive child. And it's a beautiful home. But wait. Remember what Tiffanie and her drug-flavored boyfriend said? Nicole used drugs. And there was their bait. The worst chapter in my life had started.

Long before DHS arrived there were good times. Many relationships have similar fate. You start in love and slowly, without realizing it, you drift apart. At some point most take the other for granted, throw in a major crisis, and it's all but over. Nicole was fun and very sweet at times, but also volatile. I had negatives attributes I brought, and I accept my responsibilities for our demise. I doubt any couple could survive the torture we were to encounter.

The Family and Risk Assessment had come back. The summary stated "No neglect. No danger". But mother needs to give a urine sample, referred to as a UA, which stands for *urine analysis*. The noncompliance began. Over and over. And still, I knew nothing about it. DHS visits to the house went unanswered, with cards left at the door. Mail taken and unopened. How could I know? I was working every day. Nicole, worried if I knew the investigation centered on her and Ginger, became withdrawn, secretive, and vigilant in her quest to solve the problem alone. I knew something was wrong. I assumed she was having an affair. Those were the symptoms. Her behavior became erratic. After two to three months, in late December she cracked. "We're not even supposed to be here," she cried.
"What the fuck are you talking about?" I said, completely clueless.
Apparently being backed into a corner for missed drops and appointments, she used the ever-ready "He beats me" solution. It worked. Instead of DHS focusing on her dirty self, it expedited her through Section Eight to get her out of the madhouse she lived in. Of course she stayed, because there was no violence. She had temporarily wiggled out of peeing in a cup.

For the next six months or so, the lying to DHS regarding abuse she was receiving from me was plentiful. DHS told her to leave. They thought she had. She was battered, after all. But she didn't want to leave. My home is a haven. We'd joke and call my house The Bel Aire Hotel, because it's nice and is nestled on Bel Aire Road.

When she was gone I frantically searched the house for documents. Mail, anything to tell me the gravity of what was going on. And I found it. A court order from Judge Whitt. It chastised Nicole for noncomliance and missed appointments of all kinds. And at the end, stated, must stay away from Gary DeCarlo. *I knew what was unfolding* More than concerned my Ginger was being told to vacate, I waited for Nicole to come home.

"Let's figure this out," I reasoned. Producing the document to her surprise, I stated, "I know why you concocted the violence story. I will get you an attorney." Thinking she'd be happy I wasn't dwelling on the lying, I was shocked when she rejected the offer.

"I'll fucking take care of it," she said.

It was on. "You've done a good job so far," I yelled. "Can't pee in a cup? How fucking dirty are you?"

It was met with denial, her go-to move.

"My daughter is not supposed to live here?" I was livid. "Go tell those motherfuckers you lied," I screamed.

She wouldn't. She was in too deep. She had already screwed this way way up.

For the next two weeks she acted as though she had a solution. She would get an apartment nearby, a job required by DHS, and somehow start peeing in that cup. Whatever, I thought. All I wanted was to see the documents. All of them.

Still I knew nothing. According to Nicole, the documents were either at her mom's, or in the car, or maybe at her grandma's. Anywhere but by me. Nicole had mentioned an important hearing on January 10th. A very vital one, she said. I wasn't allowed to go, she told me.

"Why is that?" I inquired.

{This family was brought to the attention of DHS when Nicole's daughter, Tiffanie Gist, age fifteen, had a relationship with a twenty-year old adult. Nicole reports Tiffanie would not return to the house to be with her boyfriend, Austin Bell. Nicole reported getting law enforcement involved and making a missing child report. Tiffanie and Austin conceived a child. Tiffanie has her own DHS case with her infant child. Since Tiffanie's child has been born, Nicole has asked Tiffanie to leave the home because her paramour, Gary does not want the baby in the home. Tiffany moved out and lives in a residential facility. Nicole has a history of drug use, and Tiffany has had concerns that she is using again. The Department has asked Nicole to drop a urine analysis; however she did not do so until two weeks later. *Children and Family Services, Case Progress Report, Alex Adams*}

CHAPTER TWO

Legal Kidnapping

1/10/19

MORE THAN THICK was the tension the morning of the tenth. Kelli, our mutual friend arrived. It meant the hearing was in fact important. For the last three hearings, spaced three months apart, Kelli would take Ginger for the day, into the night, and sometimes keep her overnight. I would come to find out these were "disposition hearings." And little did I know that these hearings would have grave effects on everybody.

I had met Kelli through a friend. Neither attached, we consorted for two years, prior to Kelli vacating a spell, for minor transgressions. Kelli had been staying with Nicole, an East High graduate and server for the last fifteen years. I would bump into Nicole with Kelli living at her home, a lower- to middle-class neighborhood on the north side of Des Moines. We started dating, and after two to three months of seeing one another, Nicole informed me she was in danger of losing her home. We agreed to an arrangement of her and Tiffanie moving to my three-bedroom ranch on a trial basis as renter and mate. It worked initially, with normal relationship up and downs. She had been with me for four years prior to, and it was a surprise, Ginger's arrival.

Ginger loved going to Kelli's. With a large house and yard in Granger, a twenty-minute drive from Des Moines, she was showered with love from Kelli, her sister Julie, and her parents, Donelle and Larry. With four people doting on her, whenever Kelli would show, Gin wanted to go.

We said goodbye that morning as Ginger, bundled up on the very cold winter day left with Kelli. It would be the last time I would see or talk to Gin for seventy days, and things would be very different the next time I would see Kelli.

Nicole, after her mid-morning hearing, had not called Kelli to check on Gin or give her the hearing outcome. The silence spoke volumes. This was different, as one day turned to two. I finally caught up to Nicole that night.

"So what happened?" I demanded. I wasn't privy to the preceding. (My name was not on the birth certificate; therefore, any inquiries I made to DHS were rejected.) I didn't even know what the hearing was specifically about. "How'd ya do? Let's hear it," I quizzed.

The questions were met with silence, followed by anger. It was the first of hundreds of times I'd be blamed for something I knew little about.

"I begged them, on the stand, to not take her," Nicole cried.

"Are you fucking kidding me? The hearing was about whether they were gonna take Ginger? You have got to be fucking joking. Get every document you have. Bring them out here, so I can read 'em."

"I can't," she said. "They're at my mom's."

"Of course they are," I scoffed.

I went to bed knowing two things. She (we) had been given one more chance at complying with DHS conditions, and there was a 10:00 a.m. appointment Nicole had in the morning. Instead of sleeping, I thought. It's time to take control, she just can't do it, I concluded.

The next morning before I left, roughly 9:15, I threw twenty dollars on my desk for her endless need of gasoline, and figured I'd better wake her for a "second-chance meeting." She was like a bear in hibernation. I could barely get her to move. "Get the fuck up," I yelled. "Don't you have that meeting?" I was still not sure what kind. There was movement. I waited. Now past 9:30. "Well, this is the exact reason I'm retaining an attorney," I yelled and headed out the door. I headed to Hope Law Firm, thinking the attorneys and my checkbook would solve this little problem. I couldn't have been more wrong. While I was driving, my phone rings.

"I told you I needed fucking gas money," she screams.

"And how are you?" I replied.

It was met with inaudible screeching. After numerous times telling me there was no twenty dollars I left, I turn around and head back home. It's now nearing 10:00. I throw another twenty dollars at her. She still was not dressed. "Is forty dollars enough to get you there?" I said.

She wants to fight. I haven't a clue why. And finally, at 10:15, it hits me. "It's not a meeting, it's a piss drop! And you're dirtier than fucking mud. Call them," I yelled.

No response.

I again leave and head to Hope Law firm, plunking down three thousand dollars for a retainer. Driving, I wondered what missing her "Last chance" meeting would mean for my Ginger. It took twelve hours to find out.

It was 9:30 p.m. when a loud, firm, knock hits the door, the kind that resonates important. I peeked out the window and knew the impact of Nicole's missed "meeting." Two uniformed Des Moines police officers and a female greeted me at the door.

"May we come in?" the female said.

Mistake number one, I let them in. My research had yet to begin. I did not know how corrupt DHS was. With disregard for the Fourth Amendment, they tried violating entering without a search warrant, the fear of a DHS encounter reduced my defiance to a whimper. I did not know the law. I should have told them to leave. Return with a warrant. Return when your reason for invading my property, my house, my possessions is legitimate. And a judge would determine that, not a thirty-year-old man-hater from DHS, one of the females at my house before, who I came to despise.

I had spoken to Kelli an hour before the trio arrived.

"Have you heard from Nicole?" she asked.

"No, and I haven't seen her," I replied.

"What happened in court?" she asked.

I told her all I knew was it was her last chance to keep Ginger home, and she couldn't have one thing go wrong.

"Thank God." Kelli sighed.

"Kelli, she missed a piss test this morning," I said.

"That is why I haven't heard from her," Kelli said.

I hung up and immediately wanted to call Hope Law Firm. What the fuck, I thought, It's 10:p.m., and I don't know my attorney yet.

"We are here to get Ginger" the woman said. The woman was Jesse Stanford, the case manager for Ginger's case. What started as a normal DHS inquiry into a pregnant runaway teen had blossomed into the kidnapping of my daughter Ginger, who was neither neglected or in imminent danger. She had no involvement or bearing with her half-sister, but Nicole was mom to both and wouldn't pee in that little cup. For that I endured one year of hell and went through thousands and thousands of dollars.

"She's not here," I said.

"That's not what we were told," Jesse said.

One of the officers asked if he could check, look around the house.

"Sure," I told him. I start quizzing Jesse for info. "How in the hell did this come about?" I asked.

"I really can't divulge that," she answers.

"What? I'm trying to make some sense of this," I said. Rubbing my head I continue, "You're in my house looking for my daughter, and you can't tell me why?"

"Nicole said she didn't know who the father was," she says with a smirk.

"I am the father. Now tell me what's going on," I demanded.

"I can't," she says again.

"You won't," I snapped.

The officer returns from scoping out my house. "You've got some really cool things," he says.

WTF "That's great to know. You guys are here to hijack my daughter, but I have cool things," I said, shaking my head.

"She's at Kelli's then?" Jesse asks, looking at me.

"Kelli has her," I said.

They start to leave.

"Jesse, may I call you Monday morning to try to resolve this, see what needs to be done?" I asked.

As they now can't leave fast enough, she says, "Yes, you can call."

Yes I can call? "What happens now?" I asked. "Where is she going to be taken?"

Jesse said to a friend of Nicole's. Her name was Stacey Van Iperen Harris. For that I was somewhat relieved. Ginger had been there before, but I did not know that not even a foster parent would soon play God. And like the other entities I was now surrounded by, she too became an adversary.

Ginger was at Kelli's. My phone rang shortly after they left. I was in my car driving and crying. I didn't know where to go or what to do. Kelli had also just spoken to them.

"Get your ass out here before they do, because I am not going to be the one to hand that precious thing to them," she screamed.

"I can't," I sobbed.

"What?" she yelled.

"I'm sorry, very sorry. I can't either," I said. I hung up. I cried some more. The two cops and Jesse then arrived at Kelli's and took Ginger like a bag of groceries. And in all of this, not one sign of Nicole. The judge signed a court order to remove Ginger the minute Nicole missed her piss test. It was like having your heart removed while awake. But it paled in comparison to what I was in store for.

December 18, Singing away prior to being taken.

CHAPTER **Three**

Stopped at Every Turn

1/13/19

I SET MY alarm Monday morning to call and catch Jesse when she arrived in her office. I felt relief when she answered. "Hi, Jesse," I enthusiastically said, thinking we could get to the bottom of this. I continued, "What do we do now?"

She says, "What do you mean?"

"What do I mean? How do I get Ginger back?" I retorted.

"I can't tell you anything; you're not the father or a party to this case," she said.

"You're joking, right? You can't tell me anything?" I asked.

She gleefully chimed, "Nothing. Until you take a paternity test and are established as the father."

Stunned, I hung up and started a petition for a paternity test. Nice I thought, I'll take this test in a few days, and slam the results right back at her.

She calls me two days later to schedule the test. "It is at 1:30 on February nineteenth," she says.

"You mean January nineteenth?" I inquired.

"No, February nineteenth," she says. I can hear her laughing inside.

"I am not waiting for five fricking weeks for a paternity test. I'm supposed to not see or talk to my daughter until after that?" I shouted.

"Don't know what to tell you," she calmly says.

"We'll see," I said and hung up the phone. Time for Jennifer, my attorney, to go to work, I thought.

The less-than-Honorable Colin Whitt, presiding over the case, signed off on the paternity test quickly, January fourteenth. I would find out in this under-the-radar Juvenile Family Court, it does not matter what one does. Completing, attending, following, or complying with all requirements carries little to no weight. Decisions made in this courtroom depend how this middle-aged man is feeling. Rollercoaster decisions made on the fly reflect how his morning is going. I would find out six months down the road, after a disposition hearing, that my "Social Folder," prepared by the case manager and containing everything I did to comply, is in fact blank. They have never asked me to fill one out. The judge makes decisions with no discretion. He had never met me, asked me one question, or looked in my folder. After these disposition hearings, taking place every three months, he issues his Findings of Fact. The second one I went to, in July, offered the most ludicrous "fact" ever. A blanket statement, with no reason or rationale of any kind. Similar to me saying I live in a tree with monkeys. His read, "The child should remain in out-of-home placement. Placement outside the home is necessary because continued placement in or return to the home would be contrary to the child's welfare." (Photocopy of court order below) This after the case manager visited my home, complimented me on it, and I complied with every DHS demand. This rogue of a man can make items up, read not one item pertaining to the parties, and not one person can ask or question him. There is one word for it. Criminal. This I found out is what I was up against.

IN THE JUVENILE COURT FOR POLK COUNTY

IN THE INTEREST OF	JUVENILE NO: JVJV244876
Ginger Gist,	
	CHILD IN NEED OF ASSISTANCE
A CHILD.	REVIEW ORDER

Hearing held on the record on 7.14.2019. Permanency goal remains reunification with Nicole Gist, child's mother, with option b as her Father Mr. DeCarlo. The current placement is the appropriate one to help us towards our primary goal of reunification with Ms. Gist.

Mr. DeCarlo made a clear statement on the record that he wished to proceed pro se and represent himself.

FINDINGS OF FACT

1. Pursuant to Sections 232.88 and 232.37 of the Iowa Code (2018), the Court makes the following findings regarding notice: Proper notice of this hearing was served on all parties and persons entitled to such notice in accordance with Section 232.88 of the Iowa Code (2018) or reasonably diligent efforts to do so.

2. This is the time and place set for Dispositional Review Hearing.

3. The date of removal from the Mother 1.9.2019.

4. The primary permanency goal remains reunification with parent(s).

5. The Social Report has been submitted in accordance with Iowa Code Section 232.97.

6. The child should remain in out of home placement. Placement outside the parental home is necessary because continued placement in or a return to the home would be contrary to the child's welfare due to

7. This disposition is the least restrictive one that is appropriate under the circumstances.

8. The Court inquired of the parties as to the sufficiency of services being provided and whether additional services are needed to facilitate the safe return to or maintenance of the child in the home. Based on this inquiry, the Court finds

   DHS will offer Mr DeCarlo the opportunity to update the social history to include his pertinent information

   Visitation will remain supervised for Mr DeCarlo, given the primary goal of reunification with the child's Mother

1

I was initially assigned a young Asian attorney from Hope Law firm. We met for the initial consultation, with her thinking it was a common custody fight. When I told her about DHS, Jesse, paternity, etc. she quickly changed gears and says, "I'm going to defer to the heavyweights (of the firm) and get you assigned to one who special-izes in such cases."

I left feeling good. I was getting a heavyweight for counsel from the esteemed Hope Law firm. Little did I know this attorney would join the list of adversaries. Enter Jennifer Russell, a forty-something, slow-talking redhead with fluttering eyelids and lazier than a koala bear. We didn't meet, which I thought was odd, but I got her up to speed on the happenings over the phone.

After speaking with Jesse I called Jennifer and got her voice mail. Then again and again. She calls me at 7:45 the next morning, on her way to court, the start of her communicating pattern. I'm dead asleep. With age comes slow awakenings.

"What did you need?" she starts.

"Um, damn; hold on a sec," I stammered. Trying to get upright and find a pen proved difficult. "That fucking Jesse says she couldn't schedule my test till February nineteenth," I said.

"Oh no, it takes only four days or so for everything to be com-pleted," she assured me.

"That is what I thought," I agreed.

"You call her right back and tell her that's unacceptable, I'm head-ing into the courtroom now, but tell me what happens," she states.

"I will," I groggily muttered. I sat my head down, closing my eyes, and thought, that really happen? But it did. It was the official start to a marriage in hell. I didn't know then I would terminate her after two court appearances, a letter to Andrew Hope, head of the law firm, and $5,600.00.

2/19/ 19

I ANXIOUSLY ENTERED the lab to be "swiped." My mood was good. The lab attendant immediately changed that. Making small talk, I ca-sually implied how eager I was to get the results.

I could see her thinking, At your age? Why?

I plodded forward, as if being nice would get my specimen tested quicker. I'm soon talking to myself. Finally I gave up and asked, "How long for the results to come back?"

"Two weeks," she casually said. She could talk.

I sarcastically laugh. "No, really" I said.

Silence. "You are joking, right?" I asked. Those four words flow freely from my lips.

Silence.

Two more weeks, and no contact with Gin. A painful blow.

CHAPTER **Four**

Out of Control

2/21/19

KELLI STOPPED BY early in the morning. With blizzard conditions outside, she encountered Nicole driving and surveying my house. Where Nicole was staying I hadn't a clue. Her grandma's at times. Her mother's, perhaps. It doubles as a teenage party spot, only the teens are her family. The same place where she told DHS she was staying, to comply with their orders to vacate my house. I was abusing her, they thought. They in turn expedited her through section eight for free housing and every other social program known to mankind. By playing the victim for Jesse, it allowed her to not be responsible, and most importantly to her, not pee in that little cup. This charade would last for months, especially after this day.

Kelli sat down in the kitchen.

I excused myself to shower and get ready for work. As I enter my shower downstairs I hear my back door open and Nicole's voice. Those two, best friends for years, hadn't made up since Kelli accused Nicole of orchestrating the hand-off of Gin to DHS. I quickly dressed and headed up the stairs. I was met at the top landing by a woman out of her mind. Upset that the paternity test was done and my attorney retainer paid, she realized how serious I was to retrieve Ginger, in the event she could not. Most would welcome support of any kind, but with a wet brain, feeling threatened, and spewing lies to DHS, she created a mini custody battle, when there were none. I stepped up to get Ginger any way possible. I didn't care if Nicole got her or I did. Anything but foster care. But I could not convince Nicole of that. She mistakenly thought I was going to keep Ginger away from her. Both ridiculous and illegal. It was clear I was the stable choice. I had the house, education, and resources to enable Ginger to live like a princess. Nicole knew it, DHS knew it, everybody knew it. It was just the way it was. But Nicole was convinced and afraid I was going to shut her out. It made no sense. It appeared at times it was me she wanted, or both of us. The cushy life she knew was gone.

With each passing day, the haunting reality of what she had done, with very real consequences, was pushing her over the edge. I would tell her that Gin loves her mom. Needs her mom. I would need help. But she continued to lie, continued to fight me every step of the way. And the abuse allegations were working. They believed every word. I was never questioned, arrested, or shown one shred of evidence, but I was guilty in their eyes. It was pure insanity, feeding into the hands of this animal, DHS. She repeatedly made any problem into a larger one.

Nicole and I had been fighting nonstop since Gin was stolen. She would beg to stay, sleep, or stop by my house virtually every day. She had no real place to stay, so I understood. She still had items at my house. But I still had not seen one document. I had no idea the scope of her lying about being beaten and abused and just how long she had been telling DHS that.

There were other variables contributing to the fighting. My father had passed away in December of 2017. He left me a small fortune. In my eyes, at least. It was enough that I didn't have to work and could wait till my Social Security kicked in. For this money Nicole lost her mind. I had bought her a car, given her ten thousand dollars in cash, and it still wasn't enough. When, after eight months or so, the cash was gone, her attitude changed. This happened around the time Gin was taken. I had a safe in my office. Thousands in cash was hijacked from there. Total amount ambushed, thirty thousand dollars.

I met her at work. Though Nicole hadn't vacated completely, I didn't care. Enter Sone Sithonnorath, a forty-year-old dark-haired Laotian with an engaging and alluring personality. With her Marilyn-like curves and savvy style, she got attention without trying. There were many things that came with her: vulnerability, intelligence, fun, whimsical, and childlike at times. Without warning she could be a mistake on Open Mike Night, but sweet and supportive she was. I would find myself leaning on her in the months to come. Knowing the nuances of myself and the case, she drove me forward when I wanted to give up. When needed she checked my sarcasm. She helped temper my tolerance from going mad.

Nicole had seemingly lost everything overnight. Along with it came unmatched rage. But my empathy was minimal. Her issues were self-induced was my thought. Ripping me off blind, another. The reason my daughter is gone, and those DHS lies, the only hurdle to getting my daughter back.

As I neared the top of the stairs, Nicole, twenty pounds heavier and twenty years younger, lunged forward, trying to send me spiraling back down. But I was ready. This was not the first time she was in attack mode. There had been several incidents. The most alarming occurred two weeks prior.

I was sleeping, or trying to, but Nicole wouldn't stop. It's pitch dark in the bedroom and she won't shut up. The themes were the same every time. "Are you seeing Sone?" "I'm broke." And "Why are you trying to take Gin from me?" At this point I did not want her there, but I wanted Gin there, so I endured the insanity. Even as it got worse and worse.

DHS thought she was living at her grandmother's. Nicole even staged a lifelike room with belongings there, as DHS would do an occasional walk through. At my house, she's sleeping by me every night and telling DHS she's abused during the day. And I STILL didn't know about it.

Until the paternity test came back, by then within a week, I couldn't see one document about anything. Nicole knew once I saw the documents, she and I were history. We were almost through anyway, but she could play both sides of the fence like no other. Fooled me time and time again.

DHS had given her the Section Eight OK. She was an abused single mom, after all. There is a long wait to become Section Eight eligible, but the abuse and duress she was under, in DHS's eyes, was not fictional but real. But she needed a deposit to get an apartment. Section Eight would pay the rent. To expedite the situation (get her out of my house and have one of us get Gin back), and knowing obtaining housing was part of her compliance checklist, I paid the deposit. The first time. But over and over she claimed she was turned down. Poor credit, no job, and prior theft convictions from previous jobs slammed her background check. After two or three weeks looking in vain, she found a place that would accept her. All she needed was a deposit.

"A what?" I asked.

"I need it by noon," she begged.

"I won't ask where the money is for the other deposit," I said. *Smoked it* "Give me the name of the landlord, the amount, and I will write a check," I said.

"No" she said, "He needs cash."

"Fuck off," I said.

As I'm lying there listening to the same old questions, she's suddenly straddling me, punching away. I feel her on top of me but can't see a thing. I push forward, slamming her chest, throwing her off of me. I jump up to turn on the light. "Bitch, you gotta go," I yelled.

"Look what you did to me," she said, surveying her red marks in the mirror.

"You're lucky, now get the fuck out," I screamed.

She did leave and went straight to DHS to show them the "abuse."

I grabbed her arms at the same time she charged and backed her up and off the stairs. This was the pattern of abuse. She would charge, arms swinging, and all I could do was grab her arms or wrists to subdue her. There were times after grabbing both arms or wrists that she would then try to bite me. I could never strike back, never jeopardize the return of my little girl. Time and time again this would happen. Not once did I strike her, and she more than was asking for it. She knew I wouldn't hit her, and because of that her attacks came quicker and more brazen. I had called 911 six times within two months just to get her out. Once I called, she would flee. I never pressed charges once the cops got there, thinking it would delay Ginger's return or further complicate this ordeal. She would show up during the day or late at night, walk straight into the house, and it would be on.

"You actually think you would try this shit if we didn't have Ginger?" I would ask. "I would knock you out coming at me like a fucking lunatic," I'd tell her.

But she didn't mind a scuffle at all. Almost welcomed them. If she had any sort of mark, just more evidence to bring to DHS. And I'm still unaware of the scope of abuse allegations. But only for one more week.

Kelli is witnessing the entire incident. I manage to open the back door with Nicole in the corner. While I was pushing her out, she yells, "You'll hear from the cops."

I've heard that before.

"What the fuck?" Kelli says.

"What?" I said, "That is fairly normal."

With that Kelli left and I geared up for work. As I'm downstairs getting my items together, I hear a feint knock on the door. Not Nicole again, I thought. Ignoring the knock, I take my time. In five minutes I head up the stairs but first peek out the window. *No fucking way* Two police cars are driving away. I call Kelli. She is en route to home. "Get back here," I said,

"What for?" she inquired.

"She apparently called the cops," I said.

"She's not even supposed to be there. She wouldn't do that, would she?"

"Who fucking knows? Would you please come back here?" I asked.

"You didn't do anything," Kelli started. "I know, but that means shit with her. Did you hear that loud pop when she walked out the door?" I asked.

"Kind of," Kelli replied.

I had heard a very loud pop. I thought Nicole threw something at the window. That was the sound. I went outside and looked, but saw nothing. I decided I should be proactive and call the police, see why they were there, what Nicole had concocted, and give my side of the story. There's nothing to hide from, I told myself. I call the non-emergency number and get transferred to a detective. I brief her on why I am calling.

"Your case has not been assigned to a detective yet; that will happen today. You may call back in the morning, and we'll know who you need to speak with," she said.

"Um, OK," I said before I hung up. But I already didn't like the vibe of this. I tried to get thrown down the stairs by someone who wasn't supposed to be in my house, and I already have a case and a detective looking for me. Just paranoid, I thought. But I also thought I have long underestimated what Nicole is capable of.

On my way to work I text my attorney to give a heads-up and see what she has to say. I did not know the following texts would highlight my attorney's incompetence and create another big blow:

Thursday, February 21, 2019

GD
Nic just called police after attacking me when I was talking to u. Probly being arrested. Didnt touch her
11:02 a.m.

GD
FYI im to contact detective tomor am, fortunately there was a witness to our argument
2:45 p.m.

I didn't get a reply until the following morning when she texted:

Friday, February 22, 2019 JR
I would not speak to the Detective without an attorney

9:38 a.m.

GD
Really? Should I hire one? Make an appt w det? Nicole just texted and said " You really called the cops? Delusional?
9:57 a.m.

JR
I do criminal Law. Just give them my number to schedule an appointments
9:58

GD Okay thx 10:03

GD
Called det. Blaylock and left msg on his voicemail, giving him your name and number to schedule an appt.
10:47

Monday, February 25, 2019

GD
Hear from det. Blaylock? 10:56 a.m.

JR
Nothing yet
Hear anything from the DNA testing? 11:16

GD
Getting ready to call her now 11:19

Tuesday, February 26, 2019

GD
Just received text from Jesse, " I do not have the results yet. I will let you know when I do. I then left another msg for Blaylock to call you if he wanted to schedule a time to discuss anything. So I have no idea whats going on w that joke of a situation. 9:46 a.m.

Friday, March 1, 2019

GD
Received voice mail from det Blaylock, said he has tried you 4 to 5 times and gets your voice mail is full. Lol Left his direct number, 237-1492. I tried him once. Got his voice mail. 5:29 p.m.

I was hoping to get a response from Jennifer indicating she may step up and get hold of Mr. Blaylock. Instead I received this reassuring text:

JR
No missed calls and my voicemail is not full.
6:29 p.m.

Saturday, March 2, 2019

GD
Hi Jenn, anyway you could have ur paralegal contact Jesse 338-8262 for test results, and det. Blaylock 237-1492 for questioning? I'm getting nowhere w either lol, and feel I'm just bothering you.
8:38 a.m.

JR
We sure can on Monday
10:01 a.m.

GD Thx
10:40a.m.

And with her last text I stopped worrying so much about contacting Detective Blaylock for the questioning and Jesse for the test results. Three days later I texted Jennifer.

Tuesday, March 5, 2019

GD
Any word on anything? 11:34 a.m.

No reply. Two days later,

Thursday, March 7, 2019

GD ??
10:47 a.m.

No reply. My patience starts to wilt. I text:

Friday, March 8, 2019

GD
Well another week soon to have come and gone. Going on 60 days since a judge ordered a DNA test. Going on 60 days since I've seen or spoken to my little girl. I have tried so hard to be patient. Tried so very hard. Each day is like the one before it. I can only assume ther is no new information, I feel I have been cast by DHS as some sort of neglecting absent father, not the taxpaying, educated, home owning, thoughtful, and caring father I am. Sorry to vent but this shit is ridiculous. 7:31 a.m.

JR
I agree. We will reach out to Jesse again. You should call the DNA place yourself because they will give you the answers of the result. 8:20 a.m.

GD
No they won't. I tried. 8:30

These texts, notably the one from Jennifer March 2 agreeing to contact Detective Blaylock and then forgetting or denying it, caused my arrest and my biggest hurdle in the upcoming court proceedings, yet doesn't match what's to occur in her only two fumbling court appearances on my behalf. Later that day Jesse finally called, confirming I was the father. After discussing how the paper trail would start, giving me access to court documents, I asked Jesse when we could meet. It was scheduled for the following Thursday, the fourteenth.

CHAPTER Five

False Hope

3/10/19

MY MOOD WAS elevated on a beautiful Sunday. With the test results back and Jennifer agreeing she would contact Detective Blaylock for my questioning, I felt small progress had been made. In actuality, there was none.

A new hobby of late had been washing my car. Now living alone, playing pool and dawdling around in my new BMW was a refuge. I decided to wash my car, so I headed up Meredith Drive in Urbandale. I was loving the new Laser Point car washes. New to me, anyway. While driving I was listening to the UNI Panthers, attempt to secure an NCAA berth, in next week's March Madness. Windows down and radio blaring, I quickly surpass the posted speed limit. For the first time in years flashing red lights reflect in my mirror. So confident am I, the game stays on as the female cop approaches my window.

"What you listening to?" she pleasantly asks.

"Seeing if UNI can get in the tourney," I said as I turned the volume down.

"Insurance, license, and registration, please" she said, still smiling. "Where you headed" she quizzed.

"To the car wash on One Hundred Fourth," I replied.

"I would too, if I had this car," she said.

I handed her the items.

Grinning, she grabbed them. "Be right back," she said. But she wasn't. Two minutes turned to five. Five turned to ten. I'm staring her down in my rearview mirror. All I'm thinking about is Jennifer. She really did call Detective Blaylock. Her paralegal did schedule that appointment. She just forgot to tell me. As another police cruiser heads to us from the opposite way, I'm still thinking about Jennifer. You fucking bitch. You incompetent eye-twitching mother...I'm gauging the officer's walk in the rearview mirror. The smile is gone.

"There's a warrant out for your arrest." Voice now firm.

"But Jennifer..." I started to say.

"What? Step out of the car, sir, and turn around," she said.

Unfuckingbelievable Another big blow. Not to me, but the implications for retrieving my little girl would last a long, long time.

A phone call. One phone call to Blaylock and there would be no arrest. No warrant. Not one remnant of anything, and this would hurt more than I thought. It was short of a major catastrophe.

3/11/2019

THE NEXT MORNING I was incensed as I walked out of jail. All I wanted was to meet with Jennifer. She couldn't make a fucking phone call. For that I spent seventeen hours in jail. Slept not a wink. Released on pretrial. It was the start of huge DHS implications. In addition this so-called attorney of mine is now on board with these criminal charges. How ironic, I thought. You're representing me on the charges you caused. All I could think was a phone call. But a bigger issue than the criminal charge was the stigma of the charge.

Sone had made an appointment with Jennifer for the following day. After exhausting the three-thousand-dollar retainer already, without one court appearance, I took a closer look at the invoices. Not only was my counsel lacking, this bitch is padding invoices like Puffy Luff does mattresses. I was also unaware of the many synonyms for filing: preparing, reviewing, processing, drafting, dictating, and responding. Even when she filed electronically, the same item was also charged under filed, prepared, etc., on the invoice. Redundant billing at a rate of $345.00 an hour. And this is clerical work! She would promise the next day that the clerical work, would be done and billed at the paralegal rate. But promises are made to be broken.

3/12/2019

I WAS READY to fire her as we pull into the Hope Law Firm branch in Ankeny. Soney and my binder of notes are with us. Heavyweight keeps going through my mind. I decided changes are needed or we part ways. Three thousand dollars later we finally meet. I'm transfixed on her over-made eyelids, her outdated wardrobe. Each word is matched by five flutters of her lids. *One fucking phone call* She speaks so slow I thought. *I wonder what each flutter will cost on the invoice?*

After the generic greetings I started, "I spent Sunday afternoon and night in jail."

"I know. That's too bad. That Nicole is toxic. Wow! You have got to stay away from her," she slowly said. *Twenty five dollars?* Adjusting my posture to upright stiff, I firmly ask, "Did you call Blaylock?"

"Who? No, I didn't. The detective?" she says.

Soney's head turns with mine; eyes meet like lasers. We're in a stare down. I am still unable to explain it. But somehow, someway, as we staggered out the door, she was for the moment still my counsel.

CHAPTER **Six**

Help from Hell

3/14/19

I HADN'T SEEN her since she pioneered the taking of my girl. I always thought she appeared to have enjoyed it. Three months three days since she showed up at my house with two cops in tow. Dressed like a grunge rocker with matching smirk, she would talk as if saying, "I know you don't like it, but I'm Jesse Fucking Stanford." Reminds one of Ellen Degeneres, with an attitude, when she spoke.

With the positive DNA test I was very excited, but I didn't know the bureaucracy, procedures, or policies. I just knew I was my little girl's dad and wanted her back.

With a brisk walk and my head clear, I enter the DHS building a half mile from my house. After icy greetings, Jesse and I sit at a round table, with open cubicles around us.

"What can I do for you, or what do you need to know?" she started.

Are you kidding me? That's what you fucking ask me? I'm thirty seconds in and in disbelief. Staying calm and clearing my audio with a short shake of my head, I said, "Jesse, you know why I'm here. Why would you start by asking me that?"

She says, and this statement and tone will stay with me till I die, "Just because you're the father doesn't mean you march right in and get Ginger."

"You are joking, right?" I asked. With my voice now rising and two large women turning their chairs to watch, I said, "I didn't come in here thinking I would snatch Ginger the way you guys did. And I didn't have the attitude that you do now when I walked in. Tell me, what is it I need to do to get her back?"

To my amazement she pulls out a yellow legal pad and starts scribbling.

This needs to be videotaped; this cannot be protocol.

With my mind buzzing she quickly blurts out, like a game show host, "You need to drop a specimen." She looks up, smiling to see my reaction.

"That it?" I said.

"No." She shakes her head. She continues to think of ways to sabotage me.

While she is writing another demand, I ask, "Is there a standard or a form, or is this made up as we go?"

With her face turning not red, but purple, she rapidly writes down four other items.

Shut up, Gary

She tears the page off and hands it to me. It is barely legible, so I ask to go over the items. They are: UA (that afternoon), substance abuse evaluation, mental health assessment, parenting class (six weeks long), and Medicaid applications.

"I have a question for you, Jesse," I said. "Why me? What did I do? Aren't these Nicole's requirements? Why do I have to do any of this?"

With Social Services jargon she said, "Any DHS involvement with parents from the same house are subject to the same compliance."

Sounds like a nursery rhyme I didn't believe a word she said but said the work would be done in a few days.

"A few days?" she said.

"Yes. It's not that difficult," I said. Holding the "contract" (below) I left as most of the workers, women, turned their heads to look.

After leaving the DHS building, I fought rush hour traffic, and arrived at a Children & Family Services building, prior to their closing to give my UA. The worker at the building asked who referred me, as they had no call or record of my name. He tried calling Jesse and got her voice mail. She forgot to call or assumed I wasn't going. *Real nice* I took off work the following day to comply.

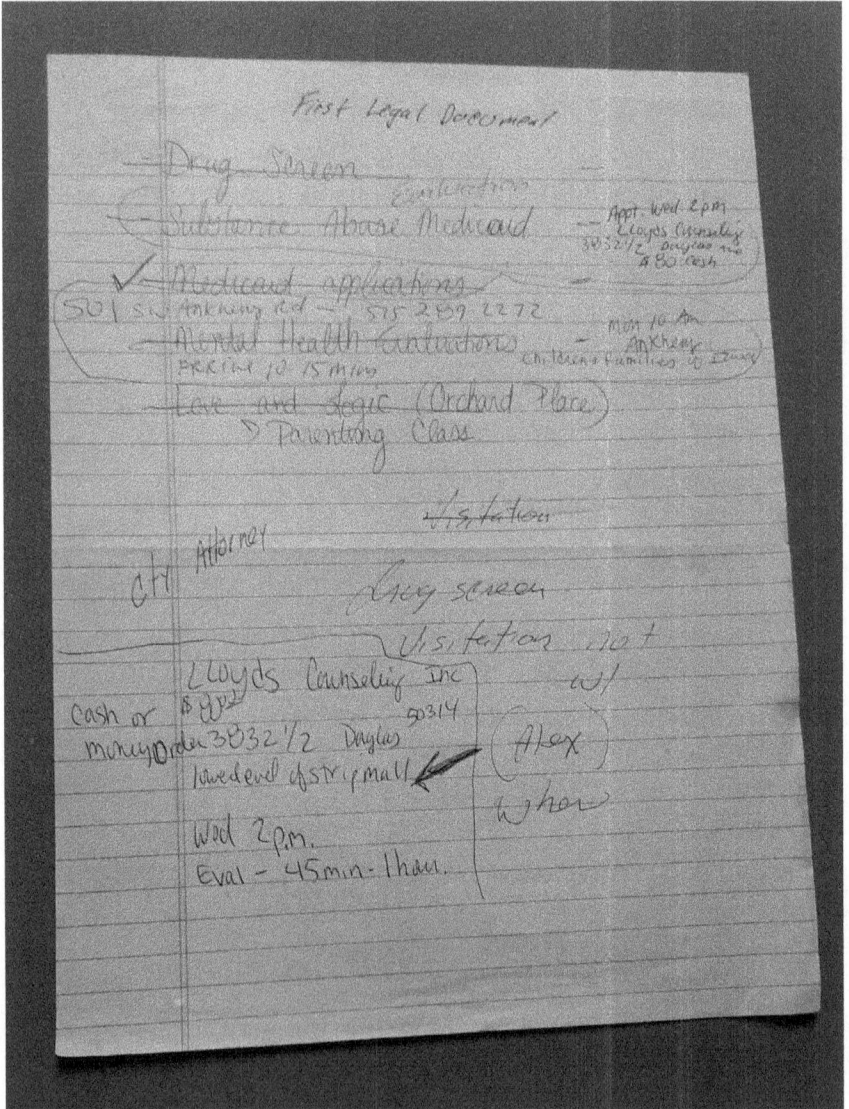

CHAPTER Seven

The Visit

3/21/2019

I QUIT MY job March 2019. I had to. Fulfilling DHS requirements was a full-time job. That's the way I did it. Attitude and composure were vital. It was becoming blatantly clear it was me against them. I had not one ally, and that included my attorney. I devoted the last three months to compliance, from forced therapy, parenting classes, random drug tests, and vibrant visits with Ginger.

There were two ninety-minute visits per week. Supervised. Excruciatingly painful. The first visit left me gasping. The last time I saw her had been that weekend of January 10. Seventy long days. I had not spoken or seen my princess. For those seventy days the one underlying thought I had, every day, was what must she be thinking? I would cry daily, by myself. I let her down. I had always told her I would never let anything happen to her. I did. It may not have been my fault, but I did. We cried for most of the ninety minutes. We ran to each other and embraced when she jumped out of the car, tears streaming down our cheeks. We couldn't let go of each other. I struggled for words, reaching to touch her throughout. *I'm hoping she doesn't ask me, "Why, Daddy? Why?"*

We sat on her bed in her newly done bedroom. We were both proud of it. I look up at this stranger in the bedroom two feet from us. This stranger is Alex Adams, supervisor for FSRP who brought my kid to my house and is now hovering over us to "supervise." I'm struggling to love my girl and not kill a stranger simultaneously. I am sixty-one. I have three grown, beautifully adjusted adult children. I now have a thirty-something white female with no children of her own supervising Gin and me, who I spent hours every night with for the last four years. *Focus on Gin; ignore Alex.* She is following us from room to room.

With half the "visit" still remaining, I'm already struggling with the goodbye. As we near the ninety-minute mark I do all I can to keep it positive and upbeat. Fat chance. Tears already flow from Ginger's perfect face as she struggles to get her shoes on. I cannot cry, I tell myself. I kneel down and say, "I want you to listen to me Gin." *Get away from me, bitch. What the fuck are you doing?* "This is a good thing. This is the start of Daddy bringing you home. Understand that sweetheart. That is what is going to happen." I look up with contempt at this...person hovering over me, as if saying "Good luck." I finish tying Ginger's shoes, grab her under the arms, and throw her into the air. As she lands on her feet she extends her arms and asks me to carry her to the car. I cannot cry.

"I don't want to leave," she sobs. The tears pour down her as we head to the car.

Putting her in the back seat as she clings to me is tearing my heart out. "I will see you tomorrow." I repeat "This is a good thing." I somehow get her in and shut the door.

The car backs out the driveway slowly. I'm now on the front porch with tears streaming down my face. She continues to wave as I blow her a kiss. She used to catch them when she was here. When she is out of sight I open the front door and slam it, vibrating the house. I am screaming, yelling, and crying. "Those motherfuckers!" I yelled over and over. Only nobody could hear me.

CHAPTER Eight

Science Fiction Hearing

4/14/2019

FOR WHATEVER REASON, I decided to retain Jennifer as counsel. In retrospect I can't think of one. Nor can Soney. Daily we would bounce ideas and opinions of the case off one another. Intuitively we were equals. With a masters in biology, she had a different perspective, a confirmation, or a dose of clarity she could offer.

Three months immersed in this nightmare two things were obvious. I must stay patient and keep my emotions in check. And my opposition was not just one agency. It was a collective front.

I had been waiting for this day for three months. A modification of placement hearing. A hearing to convince the judge to return Ginger to me. Jennifer had filed the motion in February. Maybe that's why I kept her. And she was familiar with the case. One thing I had hoped for, while questioning her intangibles, was maybe she's a freaking beast in the courtroom. I had been told she was a heavyweight from Hope Law Firm.

Two days before the hearing I'm excited. Hopeful. I want Jennifer and I on the same page. I'll do all I can to help with the case. I'll bet she's a beast in the courtroom, I told Soney again. I enthusiastically texted Jennifer:

Sunday April 14,2019 GD

Hi Jen, I know it's Sunday, maybe get back to
me tomoro, before Tue hearing. I dont even know
the time of it yet. Did you get the email I sent
you? An in depth report from Alex, the in Home
Counselor who has supervised the in home visits
at my house. It is very favorable of me, and I know
Judge Whitt needs to read it. Thinking we should
touch base before Tue. She also said there is a
motion to dismiss DV charge.

In two days I have my modification of placement hearing, I'm
nervous and excited, I have items I want to go over with my attorney.
I ask, almost plead, to meet up with her before the hearing. Not only
does Fluttering Flo not respond or schedule to meet, she texts:

Monday April 15, 2019
JR
130 court tomorrow
1:30 Pm

No shit Sherlock

The day of my modification of placement hearing was finally here.
It was also the first time attending the quarterly disposition hearing.
Disposition hearings are for all the parties to provide updates. The attorneys speak on behalf of their clients. It's essentially the parents and
their attorney's versus DHS, the county attorney for the state, and the
judge. Yes, the judge too. Hoping the judge would listen to both sides,
remain neutral, and make objective decisions based on fact would be
wishful thinking.

I figured because Jennifer blew me off about meeting before this hearing, she would arrive fifteen to twenty minutes beforehand, discuss the particulars, and I would watch this heavyweight, as the Asian colleague from Hope Law firm called her, in action. She did arrive early. Earlier than the start of the hearing. We took the two to three minutes and prepared to rebut the pending DV charge and what my qualifications were to get my Ginger back. She also asked if Stacey, the foster parent wannabe, was going to be there. Stacey at that time was in favor of Ginger returning to me.

We enter and sit down at a large table, each party paired with their attorney, as friends and family fill up the back section. It's the first time I see her folder and what she has brought. *Looks rather thin.* I had already discussed and emailed Jennifer the monthly Visitation Reports by Alex Adams of FSRP. I was surprised they didn't appear to be in her folder. As we're settling in I lean over to her and whisper, "You're sure, Jesse, the judge and everyone reads those reports?"

"Oh yeah," she reassures me.

I'm sure they are already introduced as exhibits I then look next to her folder and see what appears to be a pager. *No, that's a twenty-year-old flip phone* I'm mesmerized by this vintage device, apparently found on the way to court. But then she picks it up to check her messages. *That's how my attorney communicates with me?*

The court attendant starts off by saying, "Judge Whitt will not be presiding today. Instead the Honorable Kathy Moegen. Please rise."

Continuance I look at Jennifer, who's staring straight ahead. *She knows what she's doing.* "No problem?" I said, tapping her on the shoulder.

"I'm sorry. Problem with..." she whispers.

"With Whitt being gone?" I quickly said. *Hello*

"I think it should be OK."

What the fuck did she just say? Whitt had scheduled my modification hearing the same day and time as the disposition hearing. He had decided to deny my motion before the hearing, as to not waste the court's time with a second trip. *Very prudent judge*

I was the first to be called to the stand. The first time any of these players had seen me. But for two years they HEARD about me. They heard I was abusive. Allegedly had pictures as well. (The night Nicole jumped on me while I was sleeping and punched me, I shoved her hard in the dark to get her off me. It produced red marks on her chest and neck). But they also had that DV charge pending, From February. *One phone call*

"Do you swear to tell the truth the whole..." Jennifer's first questions were basic, giving me an opportunity to tell about myself: Iowa College graduate; homeowner; three grown, successful adult children; school teacher, etc. She then asks why I should have Ginger returned to me.

"Because I'm her father. My home is her home. The only one she's lived at. We have a bond like no other. It's in her best interest. She is regressing before my eyes. She went from a vibrant, outgoing girl who would sing songs from beginning to end, dance and laugh all night to an emotionally devastated little girl, who arrived at my house after seventy long days for our first visit and couldn't get through half of her ABC's." I continued, pleading, staying fact based, keeping my composure, and offering to do or comply with anything asked of me, for the return of my princess.

"You may cross examine, Ms. Moffitt," the judge says, as in Nicole's attorney.

With a homely look and matching presence, she starts by holding a copy of my Mental Health Evaluation. Pointing to a section, she says, "It says here Mr. DeCarlo you don't believe you need therapy." She pauses.

Is that a fucking question? I'm looking at her. After three or four more seconds of staring at me, I asked, "Did you want me to respond?"

"Well, yes," she says, as if she asked a question.

"Are you asking me if I think I need therapy?" I said.

"Yes," she says.

"No," I replied.

"Well, why is that?" She fires.

"It's probably twofold, I don't believe I have any issues, other than DHS invading my home, my life, and taking my girl, and secondly the assessment did not indicate a need for therapy."

"Is that so, Mr. DeCarlo? It says here you are to participate in relationships and children with trauma."

"Does it?" I ask. *Quit being a smartass* "That's because that's not the original assessment. Jesse and Jenna came up with that on their own. That was added or written after the original assessment was done. Ask either one," I said.

"Where do you live, Mr. DeCarlo?"

I assume that topic is over Thirty-eight sixteen Bel Aire Road," I replied. *Where is this going?*

"And why is that?"

Trying not to come off flippant, I politely said, "Because that's the address of my home."

She grabs another packet of papers. Acting like she's watched too much *L. A. Law*, she points to a section in the paper and says, "But you're not even supposed to be there, are you? Have you read this protective order?"

Fuck no "I believe I scanned it," I said. "I'm not supposed to be at my house?"

"No, you're not," she says.

"Why's that? Nicole's been gone for months," I asked.

"Because it says so on the order?"

Honey, I ain't goin' nowhere "Oh, has to be a mistake," I said.

"I want to get back to the therapy topic. Is it your testimony to the court that you are saying you do not need therapy?"

"No, I believe I said I didn't think I needed therapy. There is a difference in the two. In fact, I'm currently going, and I'm going to try to get something out of it," I countered. *Nice job cowboy*

"But let me be clear," she starts again. "You're going, but you don't think you need to go?"

"That's correct, but again it doesn't mean I won't learn anything. I'm sure everyone in this courtroom could learn something from therapy," I said. *Better stop* My DV charge was still pending and Moffitt didn't bring it up. In closing she said she objected because I was resistant to therapy.

Next up in Let's Bash Gary was the county attorney for the state. He immediately brings the charge up. "If you were convicted of your pending charge, do you know it carries a five-year No Contact order with it?" he started.

"No, I didn't know that," I replied.

"If you had Ginger, how would that be handled with Nicole?" he asked.

"I don't know, a third party, perhaps, but this charge hasn't even been litigated, nor will it. It's going to be dropped," I said confidently.

"Is it? No further questions, Your Honor", he smirked.

Jennifer was next. To rehabilitate this menace to society. I assumed she would focus on the domestic charge, like we discussed. "Gary, how long have you lived at your current residence?" she starts.

"Fifteen years, I believe," I replied.

"And you have never lived anywhere else?"

"No," I responded while staring holes through her.

"No further questions, Your Honor," she says.

"You may step down, Mr. DeCarlo," the judge adds.

I'm going to kill you, Jennifer I staggered like a zombie toward her and plunked down. She's facing the judge, finally turns, and whispers, "You did really good."

I'm both angry and hard of hearing. I'm too loud at times. I tried with no luck to whisper, "What the fuck was that?" My head is buzzing, but there's more.

The judge, like P. T Barnum, calls circus attraction Jesse *I'm Fucking* Stanford to the stand. I look up, and there she was. Again. To inflict more pain. *I often imagine God's plan for Jesse*

The county attorney starts by asking Jesse if she thought Ginger would be safe at my house. She emphatically says no, while shaking her head. I am now not staring at Jesse, but Nicole. I am in disbelief with what I'm hearing. She's looking everywhere but at me.

But we have those visitation reports

After five minutes of portraying me as Ike Turner, it was time for Jennifer to cross exam Jesse. *Here comes beast mode*

"Has Gary ever been convicted of assault, domestic abuse, or anything of that nature?" Jennifer starts.

Jesse says, "I don't know."

Pounce bitch

"For the record, he has not," my lawyer states. *That's it? That's all you got? Tear her fucking up*

I'm leaning at the very edge of my chair, trying to pull words out of her mouth. Ask why in the fuck are you opposed to Ginger going home. Ask her what vendetta or reason you people have. Ask her if Gary's ever been questioned about fighting with Nicole. Tell her this is injustice. Get mad, Jennifer. Show some fucking emotion! But instead of making Jesse come off like the biased, man-hating fool she is, Jennifer changes gears and asks about the visitation reports. *At least this will be good* The glowing visitation reports chronicled the month of visits with Gin and me. It was filled with the love, our rapport, and the obvious bond we have. It was well written by Alex Adams, who supervised those visits and was present at the hearing.

Eyes fluttering like a hummingbird, Jennifer slowly asks Jesse, "Have you read the visitation reports from Alex Adams regarding Gary and Ginger?"

"No," Jesse replies.

Get her ass!

"Why is that" Jennifer continues.

"I haven't had time," Jesse answers.

"And they were emailed two or three days ago?" Jennifer asks.

Make her read the whole thing out loud on the stand

"I'm not sure," Jesse says.

Get 'em out Who has 'em? Get 'em out
"No further questions, Your Honor," Jennifer says.
You're so fucking fired
Motion denied, of course. I don't recall anything after that. I was the first to exit the courtroom.

I heard the next day Jesse was leaving DHS for a different job. It explained a lot of things. It's human nature when you're a lame duck. Her lackadaisical approach toward Nicole. The I-don't-give-a-fuck whether you comply or not. She didn't care one ounce about my visitation reports. She was done. The same feeling I had.

My mind shifted to many things. What does this mean for Gin? It couldn't be any worse. Everything that has happened has gone against me. I get the worst attorney. I get a lame-duck case manager hating me before we met. I get a detective issuing a warrant after one day without questioning me. I get a therapist violating my trust, telling DHS everything I said in private. I get a judge who doesn't read one thing I've complied with and makes fact findings without reasons. Everything is decided. My despair is at an all-time low.

I wondered if Jesse, this her last case before leaving DHS, tried to leave it in chaos. I wondered what I would say to her if we ran into each other outside of her insulated world. I thought of a section I wrote for Gin in Time Capsule. It read, "Stand up to bullying. Bullies are the same as malicious adults. Malice with forethought is the root of all evil. They are both criminal. It is one thing to not know better. That is forgivable. It's quite another to know, plan, calculate, and act with malice." When I think of Jesse, that is what I think of.

CHAPTER Nine

Jenna the Puppet

4/24/2019

I WAS ENTERING my third straight month of therapy. At times as I drove there, I laughed or cried. DHS stole my daughter from Nicole, so I need therapy? Sounds right. They told me to focus on two themes. Abusive relationships and children who suffer trauma. I had never hit a woman. I'm being attacked in my own home. And I endure weekly sessions with a therapist who tells me I'm not taking accountability for my abusive ways. All I wanted was to get out of there. Fuck being honest. It wasn't working. That stigma. I said to Jenna before the start of our third session, "Let's start over. I'll tell you what you want to hear. Is that what you want? You're telling me women in this country do not fabricate abuse?"

My therapist, Jenna, appeared to be a recent grad, a textbook therapist. Intuition level nonexistent. I could have provided years of life lessons, had we switched chairs. Every session started the same. "Did you have a good week? Any new developments?" She loved that question.

I would tell her the week's dirty deeds. "There's more I would say. Want me to continue?"

Salivating she would nod. Some sessions I spent the entire forty-five minutes providing her week's entertainment. I only imagine her with friends repeating my intimate details after a few beers. I could tell she started to look forward to "my" therapy.

After her initial assessment of my Mental Health Evaluation, with no therapy recommended, she forwards the findings to Jesse, the case manager. Jesse soon calls me. "You are required to do follow-up therapy," she happily says.

"No, I'm not," I said. "Read the assessment."

"Anyone who is party to the removal of a child is required to partake," she says.

"Even though the assessment indicates there's no need?" I quizzed.

"Yes," she retorts.

Who makes this shit up? That was the start of my therapy.

My first session was a bit of a waste. A therapist with no knowledge of why I'm there. Awkward. In between session one and two, Jenna and Jesse brainstormed and came up with two topics. Abusive relationships and children with trauma. Astute thinking, I told Jenna, starting session two. "You guys pick abusive relationships because Nicole has you fooled. Then traumatize the shit out of my kid, and have me take therapy to fix the trauma you caused. Do I have this right?" I said.

Jenna, speechless a moment, fumbled around with two release forms and handed them to me.

"What are these?" I asked.

"To allow us to provide to DHS that you are participating in therapy," she says.

"Let's get started," I sarcastically chimed.

At the end of April, my placement of modification hearing now over, I start the session in a very foul mood.

Like clockwork, Jenna asked, "Did you have a good week?"

"No, Jenna, I didn't. I want to see a copy of that release form I signed several weeks ago, where you said it was a form to let DHS know I'm participating in therapy. That's the form I would love to see," I answered.

"Sure," she meekly replies. "Is there anything wrong?" she asked."
Wrong question "There is, Jenna. Let me explain. You may or may not remember, but I had a hearing last Wednesday. A very important hearing. To me, anyway. A hearing about my little girl. Hell, that's the only reason I'm here, Jenna. It's the reason I quit my job. It's the reason I have spent every day running through brick walls to comply with you people. And you know what, Jenna? I didn't do a thing. They took my girl from my lying ex-girlfriend. But I'm still doing all these things like they took her from me, because I love her like no other. So at this hearing I'm on the stand like I've been waiting to do. Nicole's attorney, a B named Moffitt, gets up to cross exam me. Know what she says, Jenna? Let me tell you. She is holding a group of papers and starts quoting you, Jenna. She asks me, 'Mr. DeCarlo, your therapist indicates to us you do not feel a need for therapy. Is that correct?' Surprised, Jenna, that she's reading items I told you, I replied, 'That is correct. I don't feel I need therapy.' You know what is now going through my mind, Jenna? What else did I tell my therapist in private? In confidence? Is this legal? I know it's fucking unethical. Moffitt then asks, 'Why is that?' I reply, 'Because there is nothing I have done that warrants a need for therapy. The assessment indicates that.'

'So you are denying you have ever hit Nicole?' she asks. 'That is correct,' I said, 'but I will state she has assaulted me several times. I have never been convicted of any domestic in my life,' I said. Tell me, Jenna, what I say to you in this little room, are you telling me it does not stay in this room? Are you telling me there is no sort of therapist-client privilege? I feel betrayed, Jenna. I pour out my heart, and you pass it to DHS like a letter to the mailman. This is my life. This is my little girl. Does this happen often? Do you think I knew what I was saying to you would be passed to Jesse? Did you tell Jesse I called her a bitch? What can and can't I say? You're my therapist. This appears criminal to me. I did sign off on the release. You saw I didn't read it. You indicated it was to confirm I was in therapy, not specifics. Are you guys affiliated with DHS, because I am very confused. There, Jenna, That's what's bothering me."

4/26/2019

IT'S NOW BEEN three and a half months and disturbing realizations are hitting me. This was going as bad as it could. Where is the silver lining? I would look hours every day. So would Sone. Daily we would bounce every thought, idea, and opinion off one another.

One major item was becoming clear. This group—the judge, DHS, FSRP, county attorney, and therapists—work collectively and are always on the same page. These people are very different. They walk and talk different. They have their own body language and dirty little secrets. But they are always in sync once in the courtroom. Their primary goal to suppress and maintain their rank. It's like an exclusive club they're in. Then it hits me. They function identical to a company. No, they are a company! And just like companies, they have different tiers. They have common goals.

Probably have a mission statement too. It would read like this: **We at Family Court realize the full impact we have on families, without interference, securing one child at a time.** The hierarchy of the company I battled went like this: Judge Whitt was CEO; Jesse, director of operations; and Alex was the regional manager. She traveled from home to home providing insight, lies, and updates to management. The therapists were not salaried, but heavily commissioned. For each parent they deceived who lost their parental rights they'd receive a commission. Rounding out the company are the minimum-wage employees, Marcia and Stacey. Both aspire to move up but are not deceptive enough. The court-appointed attorneys, Moffitt and Paul White, are vendors to the company. They offer up the heads of parents, like a bag of potato chips, for flat fees. Put this company-like group in Family Court and calculate your odds. There is no due process or oversight. You would be treated fairer in third-world legal systems than you are in Family Court.

Here's an example of this group acting like a company. The case manager, Tylaiha, apparently overstepped her authority by telling me I had earned overnights. It was signed off by her supervisor. (All recorded). They both backpedal or missed the memo, and Tylaiha calls me with a lame alibi. (I missed a progressive step.) Afterwards, she may as well have been sent to the moon, as I had no contact with her for over one month. Another example involved Jordan (a new therapist) and Alex. I asked both several times for a copy of the case plan after being told I had access to any document after my paternity test. Both said they would have to check to see if I could have a copy. Has anyone else ever been denied their own case plan? Who did they have to check with? Tylaiha.

CHAPTER Ten

Jennifer's Last Dance

5/15/19

THE PRETRIAL CONFERENCE for my domestic violence charge was scheduled for 10:30. I had garnered two affidavits, one from Kelli, who witnessed the incident, and one from my son, who was outside of my home at the time. In addition Nicole wrote a statement, recanting she was hit. Jennifer's job was apparently to just show up. And she did, at 10:28. I was thinking she may do some legal maneuvering, the kind you see on TV, unlike the April sixteenth hearing. I wanted the fucking charge dropped. And I wanted it dropped long before this. I had expressed the importance to her in relation to DHS, and I'm still thinking one phone call to that detective, and this part would be over. It was hindering everything. She could have contacted County Attorney Mark Sandon, armed with three documents, and had it dropped three months earlier. Her attempt to contact him was one voice mail message. I was expecting to leave the courthouse with the charge dropped.

I wait outside the courtroom while she's inside for fifteen minutes. She exits holding two sets of papers, each stapled. As I stand to meet her and read them, she says, "I got the order modified."

"You got what order modified?" I asked.

Pointing to a bench she says, "Let's sit over here."

"I ain't sitting nowhere," I said.

Smiling, she says, "The one that states you couldn't live at your house."

"It was a fucking typo nobody cares about," I said. "What about the charge? You didn't get it dropped?" I asked.

"It will be, once Nicole contacts Mark," she says.

"Let's do sit down." I started. "You just left Mark Sandon, and you want Nicole, who couldn't make a 911 call, to contact the county attorney who was just in the room you left. Can I ask what the fuck for?"

"To corroborate her statement. It's not notarized," she meekly says.

"Can I have the court orders?" I said, extending my hand.

The first was the modified no-contact order she was so proud of. The second was a scheduled pretrial conference for the yet-to-be-dropped DV charge. I grabbed them, told her this is insane, and left. As I'm driving home I glance at the date on the pretrial paper. It read August 15, 2019. Close to wrecking, I pull over to double check. August 15, 2019. This cannot be right. For three months I had been telling Jennifer what this delay is doing to my attempts to get Gin home. So far Jennifer has failed to make a phone call to Detective Blaylock in February, causing a warrant and my arrest in March. Failed to bring and introduce the visitation reports, the most positive evidence we had at the modification hearing. Failed to call one witness, when she asked that two be there. Let the DV charge linger for three months by failing to meet with Mark Sandon, stating she tried calling him once. And NOW agrees to a date of August 15, 2019, in three more months, like time is of no essence, stating, "We can win at trial." *Have you lost your fucking mind?* Having paid the firm $5,625.00 already, I get home and fire this email to Andrew Hope, owner of Hope Law Firm. I waited one week for a reply.

Andrew Hope
Hope Law Firm

Dear Mr. Hope,

In December my girlfriend and I consulted with you regarding my four-year-old daughter, Ginger, and DHS's involvement. On January 11, 2019, I retained your firm's services and was given Jennifer Russell as counsel. What started as a difficult situation has developed into a nightmare. Jennifer has appeared inept, ill prepared, and generally unresponsive. I am in dire need of support, guidance, and sound legal advice, all of which are lacking and have left me desperate.

Transgressions include:

-Not following through in contacting a detective, resulting in a warrant and my arrest.

-Ill prepared for modification of placement hearing, i.e. no exhibits, and calling no witnesses. (I had forwarded and discussed documents favorable to us and none were brought or introduced as exhibits.)

-Lack of effort in meeting with county attorney, as discussed both before and after pretrial conference, May 15, 2019, to get the charges dropped. Despite being billed excessively for preparing for pretrial conference, the only items presented were affidavits and a statement I secured.

-Not returning or addressing emails and/or texts.

The aforementioned concerns have brought me to a critical point in my case. I need these issues resolved.

I have complied with every condition DHS has set forth. My little girl is sitting in foster care and waiting for me. I need more help than what I'm getting.

Sincerely, Gary DeCarlo

(515)-729-1783

This dunce doesn't respond.

I searched for the contract I signed with the firm. In small print it read $7,500.00 is the minimum trial retainer fee. Jennifer hadn't lost her mind. She's maliciously procrastinated on many fronts with every intent of bleeding me dry. So I fired her with a two-sentence email.

A week later she sent me an additional invoice for $1,400.00. I emailed her to wipe that off or I would pursue a negligence and a breach of fiduciary duty suit. She quickly agreed. It was the last thing I wanted to do. My energy was being sucked dry. I just wanted Gin back.

A few days later I contacted a friend and attorney, Paul Rosenberg. For $1,500.00 he got the DV charged dropped in one week.

CHAPTER Eleven

As Cruel as it Gets

06/02/2019

I WOULD FINALLY meet with Tylaiha (new case manager) in June. It would be the happiest news I heard in a long time. Prior to meeting with her I wrote her this email on June 2, 2019:

> Hi Tylaiha, I know you have been busy, so I thought I'd write a quick note/update. I don't know how up to speed you are on the case happenings, but FYI, I had my pretrial conference on the DV charge 5/15. I had two witness affidavits and one written statement from Nicole that wasn't notarized (I have copies for you), Nicole's statement recanting the fact that I hit her. Mark Sandon, county attorney, said he needs to corroborate her statement before the charge can be dropped. So in the interim she is supposed to reach him, which is nearly impossible, if you have tried communicating with her. She also told me you may call her to verify the aforementioned.
>
> I have completed everything asked of me and continue to go to therapy. Items completed are:
>
> 1)   Six-week, two-hour sessions of parenting course Love and Logic.

2) Completed Substance Abuse Evaluation @ Lloyd's Counseling. No treatment recommended.
3) Completed Mental Health Evaluation. I have volunteered to participate in therapy. I have completed eight sessions as of 6/3/19 and am willing to continue.
4) Dropped U.A.'s for DHS and the courts. Results all negative.
5) Have never missed a visitation with Ginger in three months. Two positive monthly reports from Alexandra Adams of FSRP. I forwarded those reports to you.
6) I have applied for and received Medicaid coverage.

I feel there is no reason Ginger should not be reunited with me immediately. It is 100% in her best interest. I can provide for her in every conceivable way: emotionally, physically, financially, mentally, and spiritually. Though I would be available 24/7 for her, my intentions are to enroll her part time in a curriculum-rich preschool for both learning and socialization. Despite Stacey having her "curriculum," it pales in comparison to actual Head Start programs. I have been in the Des Moines Public Schools Systems and the Boys and Girls Clubs of Central Iowa as assistant unit director with after-school programs for twenty years, and I can see the effects. And regarding Stacey, it has been brought to my attention that she and Dean have been, for a lack of better analysis, not happy Ginger is still there. I can only think negative things for Ginger when thinking of that. The reports from Alex (FSRP supervisor) detail the bond Ginger and I have. I am proud to say it's unlike any other father/daughter rapport I have seen. Nicole is on board with Ginger being returned to me. All she wants is visitations, and of course I concur. Ginger needs us both. Enough damage has been done to her, and I feel she has regressed in virtually every area. It is nothing, though, that love, support, and time can't rectify.

In addition I would like to address two additional points. I have a copy of the DHS Risk Assessment done two years ago. Firstly it will show you I had nothing to do with Tiffanie and Nicole's situation. I wasn't a father figure and had limited influence, because that is the way it developed. It was also the way Nicole wanted it. The notion that I kicked her out is ludicrous. I couldn't legally, even if I wanted to. She was running the streets and gone for days at a time. Her departure has nothing to do with Ginger or me. Because I am Ginger's father, these two cases are just that, two different situations. Ginger has been thrown to the wolves only because of Nicole's inability to comply. There was never any imminent danger or neglect, per this DHS assessment. She was taken because of noncompliance. My hands were tied until the paternity test came back. And since then, now going on five months, I have done everything asked of me.

Lastly I want to address this domestic violence. If Nicole ever said or showed bruises it was for one reason only, self-defense. I have been attacked, hit, bitten, kicked, etc. more times than I can count. I have held her back by grabbing her hands, legs, or whatever I can to prevent her from punching me. I have never been in a fight, let alone hit a woman before. There is zero record for anything like this in my lifetime.

I am asking you, Tylaiha, if what is in Ginger's best interest is everyone's goal, then please intervene now and get her home. She has a beautiful home with her beautiful bedroom, her puppy, and everyone who loves her to the moon.

I would be happy to meet to corroborate anything I've written and more. I can continue counseling, with Ginger, perhaps. The healing will never end, but please, can it at least start now? Please contact me at your earliest convenience.

Sincerely, Gary DeCarlo

6/20/19

WE SAT DOWN for our second meeting. Tylaiha had replaced Jesse as the new DHS case manager, and it was a reason to have hope. Tylaiha is a late-thirty, early-forty African American female. A pleasant demeanor arrived with her. At our first meeting, which lasted over an hour, I asked what she knew about the case. She honestly answered, stating she knew virtually nothing. I didn't mind. I was surprised, yet relieved. Anybody but Jesse. I started from the very beginning and was loving it. Finally a party to the case without bias! She can hear my side without any bullshit that's been spewed about me. I took my sweet time. She appeared skeptical at times, as the story reads like fiction, but also knew this is tough to make up. Because I had previously been suppressed at every turn, my words started cautiously. I couldn't lose her confidence. We concluded that meeting with Ty thanking me and telling me there was much to verify.

Between our first and second meetings, I continued to drive forward. I would take no chances. I started recording all conversations with them. I didn't check or care if it was legal. I trusted not one of them. I had done my research.

With my phone in my pocket and recording, I exhaled and entered the DHS offices. "Hi, Gary DeCarlo, meeting with Tylaiha Redd at two o'clock," I said.

The overweight woman makes no eye contact. "She know you're here?" she asks.

"You'll have to ask her that. I'll have a seat over here," I said, walking away. *Fuck these people,* I thought.

As the two woman at the front desk try staring me down, I survey the open glass cubicles in search of a male, a sign of fairness, a glimmer of hope for any man entering these doors. With no such luck I stood as Tylaiha came to greet me. With pleasantries exchanged I once again braced for bad news.

"I took everything you have sent me. Thank you, by the way, to my supervisor, and we both commend you for all that you have done," she started.

I almost said, but before she did.

"But there are still two things we need to address before we can transition Ginger to your house," she continued.

This isn't sounding bad, I'm thinking as I rise up in my chair. "They are?" I asked.

"The DV needs to be addressed," she said.

"Dropped or addressed?" I inquired.

"Addressed," she countered.

"They currently are," I replied. "I have been in therapy for some time, covering relationships and children with trauma. Were you not aware of that?" I asked. I wasn't about to stop. My confidence was hitting the roof. "In addition the DV charge is going to be dropped. The affidavits and statement from Nicole are all that's needed, per County Attorney Mark Sandon. All he is waiting for is to speak with my new attorney. It will be next week. My attorney, I mean former attorney—I fired her three weeks ago—was trying to prolong this until August to take it to trial," I said.

"You're kidding. Why?" Ty asked.

"There were seven thousand, five hundred reasons," I said and laughed, "as in Trial Retainer, so I hired a new attorney, and he will meet with Mark next week, and it will be dropped."

"Well, then, just have Jenna email me verifying the therapy is ongoing, and get those completion certificates I asked you for," she said. "When we get those, we can start transitioning Ginger to your house for overnights.

"Yes!" I yelped. "Now I'm going on vacation next week, so when I get back that Monday, we can start from there."

It didn't set in right away. I'm sitting there waiting for another roadblock. I'm wanting to cry. "That's it?" I asked.

"Yup. I'll walk you out," she said.

I wanted to sprint to my car, call everyone who cared. Instead I cried and cried. I was emotionally exhausted. I did it. I was so happy.

But wait! Do you know who you're dealing with? After telling Gin on her next visit that the overnights were next, elevating her spirit for the first time in months, after Tylaiha came to my home for a walk through, two days before the July disposition hearing and complimented me on my home, DHS suddenly changed their minds. Nicole had whined that there was a girl living with me. Tylaiha asked me if there was. No, I told her, just another lie. Tylaiha then backpedals and says she skipped a procedure. The next step is a one-hour unsupervised visit per week. I told her I don't believe you. Nicole called you. Something happened from that June 20 meeting to the time she did my home walk through. I told her you can bypass that. I asked if Nicole was now in charge. They broke Ginger's and my hearts. Again. It was unbearable. The biggest blow yet.

CHAPTER Twelve

Above the Law

7/15/19

RETURNING FROM THE hearing I pulled in the driveway still shaking. It was starting to set in. I lost on all counts. Everything I thought couldn't happen happened. I prepared six months for this day. All hope dissipated in twenty minutes.

To start the hearing everyone walked in the courtroom except me. I was intercepted by a court attendant and taken to a closed, monitored cage. I sat down and looked at the monitor and saw everybody I was just sitting with one minute earlier. They took me to a cage. I wouldn't be able to hurt Nicole from here. I contemplated telling them all to fuck off. No, it's my little girl. I tried to compose myself, knowing everyone in the courtroom was transfixed on my image. I then hear the audio in the room say, "Mr. DeCarlo, can you see us OK?"

Trying my best to stay calm, I quickly reply, "Yes, I can." I'm ready to kill. I can see everyone except the judge. The case has been ongoing for almost two and a half years, and I still don't know what the judge looks like. I compose my myself and then my papers, trying not to shake. I keep breathing. I maintain eye contact with the monitor. I know I'm soon to speak.

The judge starts by providing an update with dates and the parties involved. I'm going to blow these people away, I thought. My voice was clear. My mind was sharp.

After finishing his update, he asks, "Is there anything anyone would like to mention before we start?"

I said, "There is, Your Honor."

"And what would that be, Mr. DeCarlo?" he replied

"Since I am fairly new to the case, may I present a brief summation regarding my background and involvement to the case?"

It was as if he knew I would say that. "Well, Mr. DeCarlo, if you're referring to the paternity or everything you have accomplished, that is all in the social worker's report. Anything additional you would work through her to present," he said matter-of-factly.

I was stopped before I started. My rehearsed and ad-libbed speech shredded to pieces. *Be patient, stay composed*

"We have fifty minutes to cover three sections: Ginger Gist, Breille Gist, and Tiffanie Gist," he started. "We will start with Ginger, so Mr. DeCarlo may be dismissed after covering her," he continued.

How thoughtful I could not believe the direction this was going. We were two minutes in and I'm in a cage, cut off from opening statements, and will be dismissed like the homeless holding a Work for Food sign. I continued to dig in.

"Mr. DeCarlo is requesting he be allowed to progress to an additional one hour a week unsupervised visit with Ginger," Whitt started. "Are there any comments or objections?" he asked.

Paul White, Ginger's attorney spoke first. "We don't believe it is in Ginger's best interest at this point," he casually says, starting to sit back down.

I start to speak up.

"You will have your opportunity in a minute, Mr. DeCarlo," Whitt interrupted.

Is it me, or should Mr. White give a reason?

Next was Nicole's attorney, Moffitt. *I can't even look at her* She says the exact same thing she did in my prior Modification of Placement hearing. Pointing to an excerpt from my Mental Health Evaluation, she says, "Mr. DeCarlo is resistive to therapy."

This fucking again?

"In addition, according to the evaluation, he has taken no accountability for his domestic violence."

The judge then addresses me. "Mr. DeCarlo, you may now respond."

Stunned, I start with, "Your Honor, I have been in therapy now going on four months. I have completed everything asked of me for six months. One hour a week is very reasonable." I was seething.

The judge then says, "Request denied."

What the fuck is going on? Is this a bad dream? I try to refocus, get a grip on what is unfolding. I'm dying to get up and leave. I know they are all staring at me. I remember what Soney told me; check your facial expressions; they can overwhelm.

The judge then addresses Nicole's status. The county attorney starts talking of her walking out of in-patient treatment facility in Cedar Rapids after only two days.

Nice, here comes her scolding

The county attorney starts, "We don't know if she walked out because she missed her kids or whether there was a problem with her insurance."

What? No fucking way! My body's now squirming all over my chair. It was court-ordered in-patient treatment. She WALKED after two days! I'm staring at the monitor. Nobody says a fucking word until the judge politely says to the DHS case worker, Tylaiha Redd, who has yet to offer a word on my behalf, despite telling me two days prior she was my big advocate, "We'll need to check on that insurance for her."

And just like clicking your fingers, walking out of a court-ordered treatment facility, in a different city with a six-month wait list is quickly forgiven. Dumbfounded, my mind races for explanations. I could think of just one: she's fucking him. That was quickly dismissed.

What are Tylaiha and Alex, the FSRP worker who wrote my glowing monthly visitation reports, thinking? They have to be thinking this charade of a hearing is a joke, don't they? I peered at the monitor trying to look at their expressions, but it was too hard to see. I folded my folder and turned toward the door, knowing I was being seen on the monitor. It was my only way of expressing contempt for the preceding. The judge, seeing me ready to exit my cage, quickly says, "Mr. DeCarlo, wait until you receive copies of the court's findings."

"Certainly," I said, as I continued to get up and exit the room.

I'm too shocked to cry. Ty; Alex; therapist Jenna; and Stacey, the fake foster parent, are all just puppets in this show. There's nothing I can do or say. And the realization, and stone cold fact that my constitutional rights, thrown to the gutter, has paved the way for the kidnapping of my daughter. They have literally stolen her. For once in my life, I haven't a clue.

7/18/2019

THE FOLLOWING MONDAY I sent this email to my biggest advocate (her words), the worker who promised me overnights. The worker who backpedaled because a noncomplying bitch cried. The worker who sat silent on my behalf as I was crucified. The worker, like all the others, without a conscience or backbone. It read:

Gary Decarlo <gdogdecarlo1958@gmail.com>

Sunday, July 21, 12:24 p.m.

To:tyl
Hi Tylaiha,

How are you? I am starting to come out of the shock of Monday's hearing. I received the findings of fact from the hearing in the mail.

I was going to make an appointment with you but email

may be more efficient. I have several questions: The judge said DHS will offer Mr. DeCarlo the opportunity to update the social history to include his pertinent information. What does that mean? Putting another certificate in a folder? Do you think it matters to do that? I was wondering about your impressions of one parent, who walked out of a Treatment Facility with not a slap on the wrist, who has to confirm child visits an hour before hand because she misses so many, has not been in compliance in over two years, and has no housing, being granted liberal visitation, with one her best friends as supervisor and foster parent? And the other parent, in full compliance in four and a half months, who has done everything asked of him, who owns a nice home and the only home Ginger has known for four years, being thrown into a room down the hall, and being denied an additional one hour visit per week? It reeks of prejudice and extreme bias. To think I quit my job and devoted the last six months for those twenty minutes. Do I have to wait an additional three months to be able to speak or are you able to intervene in any capacity? Do I have to file a motion or appeal to be heard by anyone? I was prepared to present, as you suggested information regarding the bruises, the request for overnights that turned to one hour visits, quickly and flatly denied. Am I to start preparing for a battle with Nicole, that I feel the court has turned this into? I found out Monday I am plan B. Am I in your eyes? Is this part of the case plan, of which I've never seen? Do you think I was treated fairly? There is bias on every front. What is my recourse? The treatment from the court I have received has been unjust and aggressive and does not reflect my character, however, where is my forum to reveal it? May I see the documents and/or pictures that accuse me of abuse? May I see the Permanency plan? May I have a copy of the "Social histo-ryr report," if that's what it is called, that you submitted? And lastly, despite Ms. Moffitt, Paul White, and the judge, treating this hearing and myself as though it's custody battle, shame on them. I am all for as many visits as either parent can get. If only someone, anyone, anywhere, any place, any time, at any convenience could hear me.

Thx, Gary

The email went unanswered by the case manager, Tylaiha.

After sending Tylaiha the email, I sat in reflection mode. I thought of all before and during the July 15th hearing. My random thoughts gave way to this summation; I had never hit a woman in my life, and my mental health assessment indicated no need for therapy. But DHS (Jesse Stanford and Tylaiha Redd) forced me to therapy, and I went to comply. My therapist told me I'm not being accountable for my violent ways. And tells Jesse everything I said, that I thought was private. But I continued to go, week after week, for months. The individuals who played a role in this forced therapy were; Jesse, Tylaiha, Attorney Moffitt, and Alex Adams. Not ONE of these four, emailed or made a phone call to my therapist, prior to the hearing. Yet at the hearing, they ALL said or wrote I was resistant or not fully participating in therapy. Moffitt said it, Tylaiha and Alex wrote it. There was one other who didn't bother checking about my therapy, the Judge. The one who threw me down the hall into a cage. If this tissue of lies is legal then I'm the leader of Timbuktu.

CHAPTER Thirteen

I Hate All of You

7/23/2019

MY GIRL JUST left from her Wednesday visit. As I put her in the car we are both thinking the same thing. This is old. This is bullshit. What is going on? A joke of the highest degree. She's almost shaking her head. And she's four. Her emotional regression during the visit was on full display. *I dare you, Alex, to say one word.* I can't even look at Alex. I like her, but this whole thing is disgusting. It's now counterproductive. I'm getting a new attorney. I don't care what it costs. Fuck this. Fuck these people. Alex walking through my house yawning, like she's walking in hers to go to the bathroom. My house is personal. Friends belong in my house. Not you people destroying my daughter. This is my kid, my house, and my life. How in the fuck long can we take this? We now have a four-year-old realizing how ludicrous this is. You people need to be sued. You suck the dignity out of every person appearing in your courtroom. Not only have you inflicted pain like no other, but you're now doing it slowly. I'm dying a slow death.

I now cry every time Ginger leaves. As I buckle her in, she asks me to come over a bit later. *She has to know it's these idiots* I have to tell her I can't. Some after visits are easier than others. These are starting to take its toll. August is around the corner. All of August, September, and half of October before the next hearing. Unspeakable things that never before occurred to me, now cross my mind. I am filled with rage for the pain of my daughter.

7/24//2019

PRIOR TO THURSDAY'S visit with Ginger, Nicole, because of Whitt's "liberal" visitation ruling on July 15, was able to see Gin at any time, and I was for that. If that would benefit Ginger by seeing Nicole more, I am for it. *I'm in full compliance, and the clown denies me a one-hour visit*

Nicole texted and asked if anything happened at yesterday's visit. Stacey, the foster parent, on my adversary list for hindering visits and having monetary motives, said Ginger's behavior was terrible after returning from my house. I replied, "Tell Stacey it was normal on this end. Just killing the spirit of a child. It's probably in their handbook. I'm surprised she's doing this well."

These people cause these problems and then get angry at her. It reminded me to get Ginger's therapist's name and phone number from Stacey, as the judge agreed with Stacey about therapy for Gin and me. I messaged her twice for the information. Playing God, she doesn't reply. Her lack of communication skills made me wonder if she's a certified foster parent. At one point she wasn't. I'm thinking if the father has a question or concern, logic assumes the foster parent should reply. Promptly. *Whatever*

I told Marcia (from FSRP whos supervises my Thursday visits) you people keep her from her family. What do you expect?

She asks, "Did anything happen yesterday?"

Hell no, I told her. Go ask Alex. She was within twelve inches of us all day.

Marcia says Gin's mom's visits aren't happening on Thursdays, as if that could be the problem.

I said, "She works Thursdays. She told me she has been trying to switch days with you for three weeks."

She had no reply.

They now think I'm putting evil thoughts into my little girl's head? Fuck! I don't have to. She hates these motherfuckers on her own.

At the last hearing Stacey gets up in front of the judge and says, "Since Gary told Ginger that she would be starting overnight visits soon, her behavior has really gone downhill."

Another joke right? She has my full attention.

She continues, but first sighs. "I guess, umm, maybe counseling."

Why do you run a daycare when you could be an actress? I wanted to say to Whitt out loud, "I dare you, I dare you to ask. I dare you to ask me who told me I could have overnight visits with my daughter! Oh, I see. You won't ask me because y'all don't want to be exposed for the prejudiced crumbs you are." *Fucking cowards* You don't want me to say on the record, I. WAS. TOLD. BY. CASE. MANAGER. I. EARNED. OVERNIGHTS!

Stacey, sit your sorry ass down I strained to see on my monitor. *No HD?* I spotted Dean, Stacey's boyfriend, sitting next to her. *Boy he dressed up for court*

I had called these two months earlier, shortly after Gin was abducted, offering money as a goodwill gesture. My objective was to establish a rapport. Not for me, but for Gin's sake. I also knew Stacey, being a friend of Nicole's, had heard Nicole's venomous rants about me. The same Jesse speech. I have no idea why I tried. The awkward meeting started with me inquiring about Gin. Nicole could play the poor victim like no one. And when you're the victim, you somehow are not responsible for your own actions. It's a free fucking pass. I knew before meeting them I'd get the look over. And everyone knows if you beat, you lie. Throw in thief and drug addict too.

We meet outside. I would be as harsh with them as they to me. "How much money of the money I've give Nicole has she given to you guys?" I started.

Blank stares cover their faces.

"Aaahh, nothing," Stacey says.

I HATE ALL OF YOU

I laugh. "Nothing? I figured she would give you half." *That was a joke...kinda.*

More stares.

Moving on "There's much you don't know about," I offered. "She has taken thousands upon thousands of dollars from me," I said. Trying to convey a point, I apparently was failing. Silence. "But hey, that's my problem, isn't it?"

No response.

"The first couple of months, I sent three hundred dollars with her to give you," I said. Pause.

"No," Stacey says.

This is going nowhere. Changing gears I said, "You know Nicole is having trouble with drug screens, don't you?"

Dean, as I wonder who dressed him, says "What for?"

"Why are they testing, or what are they testing for?" I asked him.

"What for?" he says again.

Oh my. "Her favorites: weed, meth, and alcohol," I replied. *Just leave. They haven't a clue.* "Gotta run," I said, handing them $150.00. Before I did, despite their lack of interacting, I said, "You know, I will get Ginger back."

Silence. "I will get her back to my home. Count on it."

Without acknowledging or even nodding, they remained robotic.

I left. *My poor, poor Ginger.*

Another occurrence on Wednesday's visit with Gin; she asked me go with her to her bedroom. After we entered she tried shutting the door quickly before Alex got in. *God love her.*

FSRP transports Ginger to and from my house for visits. I often ask her if they speak to you while driving. Of course the answer is no. She also says the radio is often turned up loud. My four-year-old has developed the same disdain for these people.

Alex is coming tomorrow. Guess what for. To start a new parenting course called Safe Care. What the fuck for? You have denied me everything and now want me to take another parenting class? None of it matters. My mind shifts, and I'm thinking how Alex hates our new dog, GiGi. I then think even my puppy hates Alex.

I painfully watch Gin's mindset as her emotional fragility increases. I can see how she's feeling and when she's wondering. I can read the hundreds of questions stored in her sad little head. Her uncertainty leaves me defeated. I can't tell her when she's coming home. I am emotionally shot. I can't give up. There has to be studies on emotional trauma inflicted on these kids. Somehow, some way I will make this up to her. I cry as I write. I hate all of you.

CHAPTER **Fourteen**

Somebody Save My Soul

7/29/2019

IT'S THE WAY I would design my lobby. Vaulted ceilings, abstract originals on brick walls, exposed duct-work, and plush waiting seats. A young and vibrant receptionist sets the tone as you enter. The name on the outside matched the decor on the inside. But do I really care? Just means a higher rate. Actually means nothing I thought as I had a seat.

After the hearing two weeks ago I hadn't a clue what to do. I was again beaten unmercifully. They were becoming more aggressive. Something very abnormal was happening. Something happened after I left that June 20 meeting with Tylaiha. The disrespect for me was grossly obvious. Too obvious. Isn't someone in the group going to point that out? It had to be more than Nicole's mouth. I would take a week or two and make the best decision I could. There were several options: give up, stand back, and wait it out; appeal; continue to represent myself; file motions to piss Whitt off; cash my CD, get passports, and flee with Ginger; or hire one more attorney and go all out.

I had plucked him after looking on line for several hours. I had chosen three. He would be the first interview. I now was entering every meeting and hearing with little expectations, just to deaden my disappointments. That's what I sat with in that plush chair. But I did know, with less than six months remaining in Ginger's case, and the window slowly closing, that quiet I wouldn't go. Contemplating those options, I would lose on my terms. In part of my Time in a Capsule letter to Ginger, I told her just that. It read, "Always make solid decisions and put yourself in a position to achieve. You owe yourself that. Tomorrow brings no promises. After that, if it did not work, so be it. You tried. Have no regrets."

And try I would. Reading the paper I look up to see an attorney chatting with the receptionist. *Do I want him? No.* He turns toward me, smiles, and heads the other way. A moment later another attorney is escorting a group of four to the door. He is dynamic, good looking, and in complete control. He's grabbing the door and reassuring them, of what I did not know. As they exit, I'm hoping this dude's Cory. He turns to me and smiles, like the first one did, and also heads the other way. *Damn! Dude was cool.* Going back to my sports page, I look back up, and it was him. Cory McClure, partner at the law firm Babich Goldman. I stand as he tries taking my arm off, shaking my hand.

"Sorry I'm late. Follow me. Soda, coffee, water?" he asks as we head into a large conference room.

"Mountain Dew or Coke," I replied.

"Sit down. Be right back," he shouts.

He returns in a minute with his legal assistant, Ashley Asberry, and introduces us as they sit across from me. I was in for a one-hour ride.

"Give me the last court order you have," he starts, pointing at a folder I brought, and then says," Give me all those papers right there. Ginger's your daughter's name? When did CINA become involved?"

Damn dog, which question?

Now standing he asks, "What's this January eleven date?"

"The day they took Ginger from my house," I replied, happy to get an answer in.

"You're interviewing me and I'm interviewing you," he says. He now is reading from three different papers. "Jennifer Russell. Why did you hire Jennifer Russell?" he snaps.

I laugh. "Hell if I know. I guess she was with Hope Law Firm," I said.

"You know they're the worst firm in town? Hey, don't tell me how much you paid her." He smirked.

"I won't," I laughingly said. "Cory, I have a question. Does Judge Whitt read the written reports from DHS?"

"No," he casually says.

I fucking knew it. "Doesn't matter what I did to comply, does it?" I asked.

"Nope; it's all a game," he says. After five minutes of rapid fire, he says, "I like you, but I can't do this. I want to do this because I know what they are doing to you. You are sadder than you're letting on. It's rigged. A game. They don't like you. How come they don't like you?"

"They all hate me," I said.

He interrupts. "Besides the Nicole shit, what else is there? What's your criminal record? I want to do this. I can't do this. I like you. You're honest. They are railroading you. Why?" he pleads. He looks at Ashley. "This is bullshit." He looks at me. "Ginger lived four years at your house before they took her?"

"How much do you charge?" I asked.

He shakes his head. "I want to do this. They don't want me to. Judge Whitt doesn't want me to. I worked with Judge Whitt for eight years. I was the assistant county attorney until I saw how much money they make on this side."

What is this guy on?

He continues, "If I work for you, I work for you. You were on time today. Five minutes early. That's respect. I like you. I can't do this. I want to do this because of what they are doing to you. I think they are trying to terminate your parental rights. It's a game. They are puppets, Ty, Alex, Jenna, Moffitt, the whole group. They're all tied together," he says.

"My parental rights? You really think that? Did you ever see that?"

I asked him.

"There's less than six months left. That will be here in no time. There is something going on?" he says. "I am asking you, you can't think of anything else there is, besides pictures of bruises, that would make them do this to you?"

"Not one thing, Cory," I responded. "And you may be right about the parental rights. That's the attitude they have toward me. All of them," I replied. "It's a nightmare," I continued. I'm writing a book about all of this shit."

"You should write a book," he snapped.

"No I *am* writing a book," I said, handing him the 15,000 words penned so far.

He grabs it and starts reading and sees the chapter Jennifer's Last Dance. Laughing, he says, "Don't tell me how much you paid her. This is well written," he comments. "Don't show anybody any of this book. Nobody!"

"How much Cory?" I asked again.

"And don't tell anybody you hired me. Nobody! Yet."

CHAPTER Fifteen

This Really Happening?

8/5/2019

THROUGHOUT IT ALL I thought the end of this nonsense was around the corner. This can't continue. It's illegal, immoral, unethical, and criminal. I am in the middle of the perfect storm, so what should I expect? The state's largest organization, DHS, was run by a director just fired, who sent state employees thousands of emails containing Tupac quotes for inspiration.

Someone or something will intervene and we can get back to living. It's now going on seven months since my baby was taken. I reflect every day. What else can I do? I'm on line hours researching, communicating, looking for that one little item I have overlooked. But the more I read, the more frightened I get. *They want to terminate your parental rights*

Yesterday, a Sunday, there was a knock on my front door. Funny how one can sense the significance, by how they knock on the door. This one said "Answer now." I did. At this point nothing I see or hear can surprise me, because nothing can be worse in my world right now. What could possibly happen that would shock or hurt me?

He hands me a packet. I look at it, laugh, and thank him. He looks oddly at me and leaves. I head downstairs to my hideaway office in the basement. *It's so quiet now* This is where Gin and I would party it up. We would eat, play, shower, get dressed, do laundry, and anything else down here before heading out for more fun. I bought her a puppy in March. Her name is GiGi. Ginger and GiGi. She's a rat terrier and more than I can handle. We always talked about getting a dog after my previous one, Louie of fifteen years, passed when Gin was one.

They want to terminate your parental rights

I just assumed she would be home now. She visits every Wednesday and Thursday. Ninety minutes each visit. *Woo-woo* GiGi goes nuts when Gin Arrives. Gin is the only reason I keep this wild, energetic dog. She's too much for me. When I drove to a bordering town to look at her, I was stunned when the owner handed me her papers. GiGi's date of birth, January 11, 2019, born the same day they stole my girl. Looking at this date in a stranger's house, I tried not to cry. GiGi could have been a dinosaur and I still would have bought her.

They want to terminate your parental rights

I looked at that packet and laughed again. CSRU, as in Child Support Recovery Unit. It's only a test, I told myself. How much injustice can one take before cracking? I happened to be picked for the study. It's a social study to gauge the victim's mind. How long can one stay the course? If you crack, you lose, lose your kid for good, because if you get angry, you have issues. Now you need therapy. Reject it, and your fucked. This is how they operate. Termination of your parental rights always around the corner.

Looking at the package I compute money spent so far. I first quit my job to comply. The job was fun and paid $25,000 a year. I have paid $19,750 to three different attorneys, $175.00 for a substance abuse evaluation, $160.00 for a mental health assessment, $ 100.00 court costs, $450.00 to Stacey, and a $350.00 deposit for Nicole. Every day I process where I am in all this. After seven months I determine I am worst off than when I started. In addition I'm denied my child's return and an additional one-hour a week visit. I now pay child support to the state, who took her. The state pays the foster parent who has her. And the foster parent who has her, I am told, doesn't want her.

8/7/2019

IT TOOK TWO days for the circus's next event. An email from Alex. The Monthly Visitation report for August. The fifth one! Five months of visits. Never missed one, nor would I.

This report changed my mindset. Finding Cory had lifted my spirits, but this report contained lies. Perjury perhaps. Pure deception from Moffitt, Alex, and of course, Whitt.

Resistant For three weeks I kept thinking what Moffitt had said. Kept thinking she said the exact same thing at my Modification of Placement hearing in April. The exact words. I was resistant. But after that hearing I agreed to therapy. Agreed to address domestic violence, because that's what they wanted. It was mind boggling. I had never hit her and now I'm in therapy. I saw no choice. All for Ginger. Sucking up my pride, doing whatever I had to do for my little girl. At the July hearing the judge should have read I was in therapy, but I knew he wouldn't. I didn't fault Whitt, as much as I did Moffitt and Alex.

I pull out my mental health assessment, and there it is. Dated March 28, 2019. Gary is resistant to therapy but agrees to address issues. What Moffitt read in July was written in March. They implied it was new, updated information. Alex wrote, "At the hearing it was reported Gary's therapist wrote an update reporting he was resistant to services but still participating. Due to this and concerns DV hasn't been acknowledged, the judge denied any unsupervised time between Gary and Ginger. There was no update from a therapist and no resistance. It was the complete opposite. They both lied. Moffitt in court to the judge and Alex in her report about me. With that new mindset, a not-so-friendly one, I called Alex to point out her transgressions. I was now recording everything, unbeknownst to anyone. This is the exact exchange:

> *Alex,*
> Yeah?
> *Can you hear me okay?*
> Yep.
> *Okay. Your monthly report that you wrote is what I'm calling about, specifically, what took place at the hearing, the disposition hearing on the fifteenth.*
> Uh huh...
> *I am reading what you wrote at the hearing.... "At the hearing it was reported Gary's therapist wrote an updated report and it says he was resistant to services, but still participating." What report are you referring to? And what's the date on that report?*
> Umm, I don't have the report...ah, don't have access to those things, but they mentioned something about that.
> *Okay, who is they? Who is they?*
> Uh... don't know if it was the county attorney or whoever uploaded it...uh...to the...uh...court documents.
> *I can tell you it was Moffit who said it. She said the exact same thing in April. She pointed to the exact same thing in the assessment, and there is no update!*
> Right.
> *I spoke with Jordan yesterday and there is no updated information regarding my therapy.*
> Okay.
> *This is all completely false. And because you also go on to say the judge denied my one-hour unsupervised visit because of it.*
> {Long pause}
> Umm...So...like I said, I don't have access to.... like, whatever, they were talking about, um... whether it was an update

or not. If it was from a long time ago. Umm...So... I was just writing what I was hearing. It wasn't...

First off, she never said anything about updated information. It was obvious to me, maybe not to everyone else, because I listened to what she said, there was no mention of anything being updated. She said and reiterated the exact same thing. Because this happens to be my life, I listened to everything that was being said. There was no mention of a new update. If there was they would say that I've continued to go and have gone and would say the complete_opposite. Instead they don't even know I'm going! And I don't mean to yell at you, but this is insanity. You know, I'm getting screwed every which way. This is another example of it.

So in my report, I do say several times. They had a chance to review that report that you're going. I mean, I'm not your therapist, so I can't confirm that you are, but I have no doubt that you are just because of what you told me that you're doing and that you switch therapists and whatnot. So I don't think there was any confusion, confusion that you were going...

Okay

That's what I understood from whatever letter that was that your therapist wrote...

{voice rising} My therapist did not write anything! There was no update, is what I'm saying! This Moffitt can get up there, pull out a sheet of paper from

April, and what, because she says it, it's gospel, even though its completely false?

So it wasn't uploaded?

No! There is no update! If there were it would say it's being addressed and I'm going to therapy. It would say the opposite. Instead they don't even know that I'm going. That's why I said to you in the kitchen. Nobody even knows what the hell Im doing. I continue to do it and do it and this crap comes up. It's aggravating and frustrating. I quit my job to address all these issues. Right. And I get thrown to the gutter time and time again.

If you would like I can send an email clarifying that to Tylaiha.

Okay.

I mean I told her over and over again that you are going so,

Okay,

And I can clarify in this report that comes out.

I want to know.

Could you speak to your therapist about maybe writing, like writing an update on what you actually are working on?

If someone were to take the time to ask the guy. Why do I have to? Why do I have to Go? Then ask him to send to you? These blanket statements you people make are completely false! What? I have to go and then prove that I'm going? Ever dawn on you people it should be the other way around? My God. {disgusted}

So...Tyllaiha should have contacted your therapist and confirmed.

Tylaiha can't even answer a question that I have for her. I don't even know what she does. And she's my case manager. And your telling me she should have contacted my therapist? You could guess weather she took one minute to do that! But STILL takes two hours to write this bullshit as if I'm not going! You people can get away with this shit? I don't even know what she does. This is like Stacey, I asked her what the therapist's name and number is, because Stacy gets up and recommends that Ginger and I go to therapy. Okay, I'll do that too! I asked her, and she didn't even answer. I mean this is the kind of bullshit respect that I get from every entity and this entire case all the time for seven months. It is frustrating you know, and I don't mean to take it out on you, but look at it from my perspective.

{meekly} I understand.

I have complied with everything, and can't get a one-hour visit because of a false report that Moffitt gets up there and talks about. Nothing was uploaded! Nothing was updated! What the...

So...then

Paul White gets up and says we object at this point to the one-hour unsupervised visit. He doesn't even give a reason! Judge denies the request. Before I could say a word. Shut me down. This is another example of all the bullshit. It is unreal, if you look at from my perspective it is so twisted. It's unreal. You know... the wording, Gary's therapist who wrote an update, wrote an update reporting with resistance... Number one. There is no additional report! Number two. I'm not resistant! Unbelievable! And then you write this shit and because of this the judge denies the unsupervised visit with my little girl!

Well, I thought that's what he said. And I mean they were concerned. I mean there were concerns from other people that like it wasn't sufficiently being addressed.

Says WHO? Tell me WHO starts this bullshit. WHO is my question. That's why I'm calling, because I'm addressing it. So WHO started this bullshit?

I don't know, Gary. This is just everything that I heard in the courtroom. I think you may be able to have access to what exactly what was said in the courtroom because they have the court document-type person.

I can remember what was said. The word update was not used.

Okay, I apologize. But that's the way I understood; that's the way it was phrased in court, so that I understood it. And unfortunately I cannot change what was said in court about this, You know what I'm talking about, that Moffitt said it. It was Nicole's attorney.

She said the exact same thing. I'll bet you she was reading from April's assessment, my second or third week into therapy, when I'm now over four months of going, there's no update. Can we find that out?

Yes. I can talk to Tylaiha and see if, I'm sure she has access to what is going on.

I apologize for yelling at you; it's frustrating for me with the misconceptions, and the perceptions of me being 180 degrees dead wrong. I don't even know what judge Whitt looks like! He's never even asked me a question. This is the kind of respect. I go through brick walls to try to comply. And when I get hit with something like this it's too much, I have to fight back. You know, I can't continue to let this shit go.

(long pause) All right, I'll see if she'll speak to your therapist to get an accurate update. Okay?

All right. Okay. Thank you. It would be nice if the judge could get an update as well, (laughing) if he even reads it.

Yeah, so if she does get an accurate update, I can request that she uploads it to the court. Okay.

Thank you.

Okay.

Yep, bye-bye.

8/13/2019

AS I ENTER Children & Families of Iowa for yet another forced therapy session, I looked forward to the response from my new therapist, Jordan Plummer. Jordan, Jordan, where have you been? Are you fooling me too? Be honest; I have learned a lot in seven months. It's been learn-as-we-go, but I've learned nonetheless. Let's hear it before we start. Are you a traitor too? Are you like your muskrat colleagues? Y'all walk around like your untouchable, acting mild-mannered and talking in whispers. When you guys get home and your partner, or spouse is pissed, you act just like those in your office. But you, my man, appear a bit different. Can't put my finger on it, but integrity is hard to fake. Cory said to me, your interviewing me and I'm interviewing you. Well, Jordan, you're sizing me up and I'm sizing you up. It doesn't matter what's on those framed papers on the wall. Titles mean little, Jordan. It's only a sheet of paper. I have one too, except I don't know where mine is. Probably in a tote in the rafters of the garage.

He appeared very receptive. Appeared to believe all I was saying. Appeared to see this is breaking my heart. And I appeared skeptical. I left with him telling me one of his goals will be to set the record straight in the courtroom. The best I could hope for. But words with these birds fly very, very cheap.

CHAPTER **Sixteen**

Cory, Please Buy Me a Drink

8/20/2019

THREE LONG WEEKS I waited for Cory to get back from vacation. He took his son to prep school. Maybe he said private school. I could tell he was the dad most kids would want. He spent the first five minutes of our second meeting talking about two passes his son caught in an eighth-grade football scrimmage. I imagine how happy Cory will be when his son graduates from law school in ten years. In those five minutes I realized what it was. His passion. You can't feign, teach, or simulate passion. I had that kind of passion once. I want it again.

I had written down many items and questions to present at the meeting. Despite feeling I couldn't find better counsel, I knew it wasn't "I found him, here's a check, let's get her!" And ten to fifteen minutes into the meeting I realize I am still in one fucked-up situation. He pondered again out loud. He had never seen a case in Whitt's courtroom where bias was so determined. I needed a personality transformation, he mused. They may not like my competence, confidence, and drive. Well, that was obvious. They don't like one thing about me. I'm pushing them too hard, he implied. My verbal battles must stop. You may be smarter than them, he said. "Shut up," he told me more than once.

A half hour into the meeting I know there is no concrete game plan. There is no magic hidden in his office. He's thinking while

82

talking. My mind wanders to Ginger. I love her so much. He mentions Bridge order several times. Amy, a different assistant he brought, scribbled notes and listened. As he's speaking he's looking to her and occasionally at me.

I'm losing my fire with each passing word. I think of Ginger again. I want to be alone with her. Kiss her and hold her. I want to tell her how sorry I am. I want to tell her this will never happen again. I imagine her never leaving my sight. I think of all I have done and how so little's been accomplished.

"Can you do that, Gary? Gary?"

"Oh, I'm sorry. What's that?" I asked. I hadn't heard a word he said the last five minutes.

"Can you lay low?" he said.

Not knowing what he was talking about, I said, "Of course I can."

I look at my list of questions in front of me. They are meaning less and less. Without luck I try to formulate a question. I look at the time, and one hour has lapsed.

"So you email Tylaiha just a one-sentence question. Okay?" he asked.

"Yeah, and what am I asking her again?" I said.

"The Social folder. To update the Social folder."

"Yeah, I know," I said as I headed out the door.

I start the car wondering what we accomplished. I can't think of one thing.

8/27/2019

I WAKE UP wondering about the case. I had to have missed something, but I was blessed with an extraordinary memory. If there's meaning, I may recall every word spoken in lengthy conversations. I didn't miss anything. There was no plan or specified action. The one item Cory told me to do, I did: request and pick up my mysterious social folder, the one that's never been read or seen. I emailed Tylaiha, and surprisingly she responded. I asked to pick it up at the front desk. I get there and inquire if anything had been left for me. The receptionist said no and tried calling Tylaiha. A shot of adrenaline hits me as I may be speaking to a person for whom I have little respect. I was relieved she didn't answer, thinking my disgust would be conveyed.

The department did give me the packet, courtesy of her supervisor. Without looking at it I tucked it under my arm and headed home.

I was now having to gear up mentally to tackle anything case related. I finally open it, and it's more pathetic than I envisioned. This is the fucking social folder? This is shit. It's not a social folder, it's a questionnaire designed to make you incriminate yourself and then throw you under the bus. I'm now glad I never filled one out. I'd probably be incarcerated. Here's a sampling of a few questions: Who do you do drugs with? How much do you use each time you use drugs?

I'm thinking anyone who would answer those questions, is not fit to be alone. They have a section on housing history. Where have you lived in the last five years? They have TEN spaces to fill out the addresses and landlords. Another amazing one: When you were growing up, where did you live?

I read it three times. I'm still not grown up. Could it read, Between the ages of five and seventeen, where did you reside? And these are the contemptibles controlling my kid's life. I can't even think of answering half these questions. They did save the best question for last. It read, How can DHS help you overcome these difficulties?

After reading the questionnaire I shot Cory an email stating it was time to talk. Time for action.

CHAPTER Seventeen

Sad Songs Say So Much

8/28/2019

THIS TIME EVERY week I'm sad, Wednesdays around 11:45. Just said goodbye to Gin after our visit. She said two things today that killed me. One was she didn't want to leave, but I've heard that before. She says that often. But she said something she's never said before. She asked if she could take something I bought her home.

She didn't mean to say it. It took everything I had not to look Alex down and say, "Are you motherfuckers happy now?"

I have tears in my eyes. But what would you expect? Month after fucking month. I am so pissed and sad right now. After she asked, I said, "Of course you can, sweetheart, but this is your home." But with each passing week words have less ring. She's heard it all before.

This is so wrong on every front. DHS destroying my life with Ginger. And I haven't done one fucking thing. We should be playing, laughing, interacting, growing, and shopping. And it continues to get harder. I have this suspicion they are just patronizing me. Just keeping me at bay until the one-year mark. Then surprise, we move to terminate your rights. And to think I still know nothing. I don't know what the October 14 hearing will center on. I don't know about the looming permanency plan. I don't know Cory's plan. As I sit here, seven and a half months in, I realize I don't know shit.

8/31/2019

IT'S SATURDAY OF Labor day weekend and there's just one car in the parking lot. I pull in and park next to the shiny black Corvette. I wondered if that was Cory's car the last time I was here. With my blank questionaire and list of questions I enter the empty law office. I hear echoes of my steps as I look for signs of life. I quietly rang a bell sitting on the reception desk. Out jumps Cory shadowed by his beautiful gray dog, perhaps an Airedale. I prepared for the colossal handshake this time. He seats me in a conference room, takes my order, and with dog in tow states he'll be back. I worried that Saturday was invading his long weekend, but he quickly put that to rest. Smiling he enters our room and sees the blank questionnaire in the middle of the table. "I'm glad you didn't fill that fucking thing out" he starts.

"It's bullshit," I said.

"It's a trap," he says.

We go over the questions on my social history, stopping to put asterisks by ones requiring more thought. Going back and forth we try covering several topics at the same time.

He then starts speaking about the injustice of my case, how he's getting emotionally attached the more he reads. Says perhaps because he prides himself on being a dad.

Intentional or not he then starts talking about legalities of the DHS actions. A disregard of the law, the violation of my parental rights. He mentions if these actions are done with...

"Malice," I yelled.

"Bad faith," he said, then there's something there.

As in lawsuit? I kept quiet.

His mind easily wanders as there's too much info in it. He quickly changes the subject, implying we were getting ahead of ourselves, but it's what I've been thinking and saying. Their actions are malicious and criminal and violate my civil liberties. But all I want is my Ginger back. That's my only focus.

"May I be honest?" Cory asks.

"Well, yes," I said. "If you were thirty-five and everything was the same, you would be looked at as a hero. You would have her back now," he said.

"I'm aware of that; well aware age may be a factor. But I also don't have to scramble for daycare. I can be home 24/7, I can."

Cory interrupts. "I know, I know. I'm just putting it out there."

We talk of how important the October fourteenth hearing will be. At times I'm confused with Cory's many ideas. I'm looking for somewhere to hang my hat, a specific game plan to focus on. When my confusion is conveyed, he will always say, "Trust me."

I do. He told me to work on the questionnaire and he would call me Wednesday, on his way back from Omaha. The meeting boosted my bounce as I left his office.

9/2/2019

LABOR DAY, A breezy but beautiful seventy-five degrees outside, I decide to wash my car, though it doesn't need it. I have to get out of this house. As I'm driving around this holiday, cars in bundles surround houses. Little kids in yards throw footballs.

I wonder what Gin is doing. I think of calling her later, but it always turns out sad. I think how Whitt denied me one fucking hour. I could shoot over there, scoop her up, and hit two stores and a fast-food drive-through. I can't even fucking do that? It's so sad.

After washing my car I went to a couple of stores. Thinking of fall I bought Gin a few items, including a cute little flannel shirt. I already know what will happen with that. She'll come over on Wednesday, try it on, love it, and thank me. I will ask if she'd like to take it to Stacey's. She will say no. I will hang it in her closet, and there it will sit. She has the cutest wardrobe waiting for her. I buy her things, my friends buy her things, and she does not want to take one item from here. I know what she's thinking. The less I take the sooner I'll be back. I wonder how many items will be outgrown by the time she's here.

I sit alone in my house; pictures of Gin surround me. Everything I see reminds me of her. I have to stop now, as I sadden with each typed word.

9/4/2019

AS I WAIT for Gin to arrive it reminds me to complete my will. Is there a small way to make up for this injustice she has been handed? It wouldn't make it fair to my three grown children.

I have lived with a belief that fuels my perspective in life. Would you rather be treated equally or fairly? It's fairly with me. We're not all equal. I treat people based on their merit. How they treat you. Out of the three, only my son Mitchell knows the full impact this has had on me. My oldest daughter, Angela, lives in North Carolina. Emotionally I have always been the closest with her. She's a true success story. Left her momma's nest at eighteen and went to Florida for college without knowing a soul. Finished with a paralegal degree. She's also a tax preparer, dabbled in real estate, went to nursing school, and is currently a dental hygienist. Owns her beautiful home in Concord with two beautiful children.

It was a terrible visit. One of the crushing ones. The kind that when it ends, your spirits are gone. Part of your soul has left and you don't know if you'll get it back. As I buckled her up, Gin sadly said it was a bad visit. I know she didn't mean it. What she was trying to say was this is fucked up. She stated she wanted to stay again. Yes, it must be 11:45 on Wednesday. In ninety minutes we painted her fingernails, made macaroni and cheese, read her a *Fancy Nancy* book, gave GiGi a bath, hit tennis balls, squeegeed my windows, and played on the swing. Sound like fun? Not if you have to leave. Not if your life's on hold. It's almost worse than not coming. All it does is make you angrier and remind you of what's been ripped away. Yes, must be around 11:45 on a Wednesday.

The sadness looms prior to parting.

9/5/19

AN AMAZING TEXT arrived ten minutes before Gin. I'm thinking Stacey got the name and number of Gin's therapist that I asked for twice. It was instead a request for $300.00. She said she spent it on Ginger for clothes for preschool. *Come again?*

I started to reply but didn't. I laughed aloud thinking two things. Who spends $300.00 on a four-year old for preschool, and wouldn't enrolling her in preschool come first? It never happened while at Stacey's.

After Gin left I got out my phone and thought of my reply. There are two things going on; What I would like to say, and what I should say. But I decided why spend energy engaging with any of this. I packed up some fall items I bought Gin, and put 100.00 in her backpack. I texted Stacey telling her that and suggested our lines of communication should be better. Her reply: k ty. *That's the spirit*

I assume Stacey is reimbursed for any expenses related to Gin. I assume she is certified. I would find out I assume too much.

9/10/19

AS I SIT in my office this Tuesday morning, I go over dates, notes, and numerous pages of court documents as I do quite often. I receive a call from a very nice woman named Monica. She facilitates family team meetings. I had spoken to her months ago when she tried scheduling one for me. She was unable to, because the parties were unable to reach an agreeable time. The fact the meeting was for me was likely the reason, an egregious example of bad faith. The fact I had never been asked to fill out a social history, the most basic fundamental item a parent provides to DHS and the courts, going on eight months, is another pattern of bad faith. When I mentioned this to Monica she said, "I thought they were required to have that filled out. I have never heard of that before."

Welcome to my torment

She went on to say I would be given five uninterrupted minutes to address the parties at this meeting. I'm sure Cory and I will go over how I should address the parties. I know my best behavior is needed. These meetings are scheduled to allow the parties, in a round-table forum, a chance to discuss strengths and weaknesses and agree on the direction of where were going. Every proceeding is redundant for me, as nothing ever changes. Comply, comply; deny, deny. But one thing from Cory that helps; he says "Trust me" over and over.

I met with my therapist Jordan today. I like Jordan. But I've liked many of the parties until they debone me like a fish. Today will be my sixth meeting with him. That's in addition to twelve I had with Jenna the puppet. A week ago Jordan had given me my first copy of my own case plan. It took only eight months to get it. The case plan is a detailed synopsis of everything going on, with all the parties, written by the DHS case manager. He had given me April's case plan. These case plans are updated right before the disposition hearings. It is intended to give the judge insight into the deadbeat parent's progress. Understand that with DHS you are a loser, abuser, or drug addict. As soon as you're labeled (may be the first day you meet), the case plan will be filled with exaggerations, embellishments, and lies. An example is my July third case plan, written for my July fifteenth disposition hearing. Tylaiha, my case manager who authored the report, states, "Gary needs to demonstrate that he can consistently participate in services."

I don't have a masters in social work, but if a lay person (and judge) read that, it would imply I don't attend or that I have spotty attendance. On the date (July 3) the report was written, I had attended four straight months of weekly therapy. Not only have I gone to therapy when none was recommended, but also the months I have gone are disregarded and lied about. As of this writing not one person called to inquire about my therapy, specifically Tylaiha and Alex, yet both wrote negative summaries about it.

My attorney doesn't think they are playing fair. Tells me they want me to go away. Cory and I are ex-athletes. We don't go away; we fight harder. We often use sport metaphors when talking. I asked Cory if someone cheats or acts in bad faith, or doesn't play by the rules, aren't they heavily penalized?

He smiled and said first things first.

After speaking with Monica I called Cory. He asked me to come to the office. He was set to fly to London with his wife for two weeks. We last spoke after I received the trap papers, the social questionnaire from DHS. Cory had entered an appearance a week ago, indicating he was my counsel. With it came access to all documents and the ability to start calling the shots. This family team meeting, Cory says, allows us to have them all in front of us, see who has what, who's been lying, who the negligent ones are, and who in the fuck is responsible for violating every civil right I have. If that couldn't make me feel better when I left his office, then nothing could.

9/16/19

NICOLE KEEPS TEXTING saying we need to talk. I arrange a time, and it never happens. In her texts she's despondent, depressed, and stating she can't comply. It's why I got involved as soon as Gin was taken. Nicole is all over the map. There's no way she can comply with what DHS is demanding. I knew it, and she knew it. I want to meet, be understanding, tell her to tell DHS just that. Let me have Gin, and let's move on with our lives. She could see Gin anytime. Gin would have anything she needs.

There are two things that keep Nicole fighting this losing battle. Her obsession with Sone and the life she knew at the Bel Aire Hotel being a distant memory. She fucked up. We all fuck up, and all we can do is move forward. But how she feels and what she says to DHS is never the same thing. It's always a contradiction. I took no stock in what she said.

9/20/19

KRISTI TRAYNOR, AN attorney who worked as an assistant attorney for the Iowa Justice Department had recently been hired by Cory. He introduced us prior to my leaving the last meeting with him. He told me to work with her while he was vacationing. She would help me fill out the very important Social History Form that had never been completed. All I'm thinking while driving home is about her credentials. The pure luck of finding this law firm. Cory taking my case when he hand picks only the ones he wants. He had mentioned to me what a good job I did when I initially inquired seeking their counsel. You have to provide a written synopsis of what your legal problem is. I wrote exactly what had happened in detail. I thought it was too long, but it caught the eye of Ashley, his assistant, and they invited me in for the initial consultation. It became clear how fortunate I was when I did meet with Kristi. She first told me that any communication with DHS needs to be done with a "soft sale."

"Really?" I said, thinking what a hard stance I had taken with them since day one. I had always been polite, but as the months of bullshit continued, my frustration inevitably surfaced.

"They are just social workers," she told me. "They do not want confrontation."

"Jesus; that is the first time I've heard that," I told her.

We chatted for an hour on how best to answer the trick questions and make it appear it was all my doing. I was to come in the following Monday to complete it in my handwriting and then turn it in to DHS.

Before I left I asked her about Cory. I hadn't a clue who he was before entering the law firm two months ago. "Kristi, Cory is really good, isn't he?"

She nodded. "How did you find him?" she asked.

"Online is all. I told my girlfriend after the first meeting I may have stumbled onto the best person I could have hoped for," I said.

"You did," she added. "Everyone likes Cory. Judge Whitt loves Cory. He's very calm in the courtroom while assessing things as they unfold. But he can be fiery when he needs to. He is a big advocate for kids and dads."

Becoming misty-eyed I thanked her and left, hoping things were starting to change.

The family team meeting had been scheduled for October eighth, one week before the disposition hearing. Those two meetings will determine many things in the remainder of my life. Ideally and self-ishly I want Gin in my house under my guidance. I want to give her a foundation she can use, to catapult her to heights, she has yet to dream of. I have an innate gift to do that. I want her to grow in every conceivable way. After exposing her to all that's in front of her, she may choose the path that comes calling.

I have never for one second doubted the love Nicole has for Ginger. I want Nicole to play an important role in Ginger's life, but there are concerns as well. Income, or lack of it, presents a huge problem for Nicole. In the event Nicole is granted Gin, the trickle-down effect of moderate income can be enormous. Unfortunately housing, education, clothing, food, transportation, extracurricular activities, social events, and many other items have a direct link to income. Or they can.

I will help, no matter where Gin ends up. Thoughts of a never-ending custody battle is not on my agenda. It's the last thing I want. But it will be based on what I perceive to be in Ginger's best interest.

9/23/19

I JUST LEFT a follow-up meeting with Kristi. Completed my Social History Form and turned it in to DHS. But before I left, in bounced my man Cory straight from his vacation in London. I get excited when I see him. Before reassuring me this will all be good, he starts talking how hard it is driving on the left side of the road in Europe. Said a taxi driver told him you'll be fine after an hour of driving. He replied, "I'll be dead by then." He says he has a golf outing with Judge Whitt October 12, two days before the important disposition hearing!

Excuse me. I'm thinking I may have picked the best attorney available, though it doesn't mean a thing yet. But as Jack Nicholson said in *One Flew over the Cuckoo's Nest,* "It sure in the hell don't hurt none, does it?"

I then rushed home to meet with Alex, the FSRP worker providing a parenting class for me. We covered items and questions like, "When and why would you give Ginger a bath?" And "How would you show Ginger how to wash her hands?"

Feeling good I was provided with new, age-appropriate information, she asked before leaving if I had any questions. I said yes, "Who keeps dropping the ball on Ginger's dental appointments? And who has Ginger's medical and dental records, along with the names of her dentist and pediatrician? And is she up to date with immunizations? Then I stopped. "Alex, don't worry about that information; my attorney will address that and more at the family team meeting on the eighth." *Now please leave. Please.*

Two meetings in two hours. One with more newfound support than I could dream of. The other with Alex, an enigma to me. She is competent and bright, but like all state employees, is programmed to perform robotically, without regard to individual circumstance.

In three weeks the hearing will be here. Cory's goal is to have her returned to me that day. I try not to think about it. I try not to imagine it. I've been hurt so bad for so long. I don't have any pain left to give. He told me this before his vacation. I make a concentrated effort not to believe it will happen, because then I can shield myself from the hurt they inflict.

In three weeks it will be nine months since they kidnapped my girl. Have a soft sale, Kristi keeps saying. I've never had more contempt for a group as I have for this one. And I'm told to soft sell, be nice, smile, and show not a hint of anger.

I have twenty-one days to prepare for this facade. I can do it. I have to do it. My princess is counting on me.

10/2/19

I DON'T KNOW what to feel. I'm happy, possibly ecstatic. Gin just left from our Wednesday visit. While she was here Tylaiha showed up unannounced. *Look what the cat dragged in* She is supposed to visit my house at least once every thirty days. It's the first time I have seen her in person since the July disposition hearing. I opened the door and she said hello. I realized it's more than she said on my behalf at the hearing. Being pleasant while feeling undermined is no easy task.

But this is the new Gary, the Soft Sale Gary.

Throughout this ordeal on every court order, issued after every disposition hearing, the judge would reiterate Nicole was option A, I was option B. It started and stayed that way because, as Kristi explained legally, my name was not on that birth certificate when she was taken. I assumed it was a matter of time before that would change. Nicole's inability to comply and the fact that I had completely complied made my camp confident it could be argued to Judge Whitt. This is insanity. We weren't the only ones thinking this.

The first topic Tyliaha spoke of was changing Nicole and me in the case plan report she was preparing for the upcoming disposition hearing, making me option A for Ginger's return. She looked at me as though I should act like I won the lottery. Instead "It's about fucking time" was written on my face.

After they left I cried. For Ginger. There's no forgiving what they've done. I thought of everything they have put everybody through the last nine months. And it's not even over, not even close. From the day they kidnapped her I have imposed my will with every ounce of fortitude I own. The bad faith exhibited toward me since the theft of Ginger will not be forgiven or forgotten. What unfolds in the next two weeks with the Family Team Meeting, followed by the nine-month disposition hearing will determine my recourse, vindication or legal action.

I have been told the fact that Nicole has been option A put me in a waiting scenario, despite the fact I was the viable choice. It was allegedly the last hurdle to recapture Ginger.

I immediately emailed Cory and Kristi after Tyliaha left, telling them about the option switch. Kristi's response, "That's great news, Gary. We hope to hear the same recommendation at the hearing next week." Bad faith? My attorneys won't believe it till they see and hear it.

CHAPTER Eighteen

Circus Attractions

10/8/19

I SLEPT MAYBE an hour. Not that I wondered how the Family Team Meeting would go, but more about seeing the people in flesh who have done this terrible deed. As I'm driving to the same building where I encountered Jesse F. Stanford and given that conditional scribbled sheet of paper, this was way too early for me.

Cory calls. It's 7:35, and I don't function until noon. My blood-shot eyes look in the mirror as I answer.

"It is in writing," he starts.

"What's in writing?" I mumbled.

"The switch. You are option A," he says.

"I told you it would be." I yawned.

And then he says, "Look, I don't mean to be an asshole—"

"But shut up?" I interrupted.

"Well, pretend you're at church," he says. He asked what Nicole's reaction will be, then her attorney's.

"Go off like rockets," I replied.

"I'll be in the lobby," he says before hanging up.

I walk into the building faking I'm alive and full of vigor. The truth being I was depressed by entering this DHS building from hell. At ten till eight Cory, Kristi, and I gather outside the meeting room chatting with only a few others in sight. I see Tylaiha approaching. She smiles and walks by us.

"Who's that?" Cory whispers.

"Ty," I mouthed.

He immediately runs to catch up with her, introducing himself like a long lost cousin.

We enter the room and wait for others to come. Moffit, Nicole's attorney and scary in person enters.

"Who's that?" Cory whispers.

"Moffit," I mouthed.

He jumps up and introduces himself. Her reaction echoed her looks. While Cory is all over the place, the rock is Kristi, composed, unassuming, yet full of knowledge. I sat next to her, ready to scribble her notes or questions when needed.

Sitting down I look toward the facilitator, Monica, at the front of the room. Behind her on the large board I see my name, categories of strengths and weaknesses. There are underlined headlines like goals and objectives, words of therapy, counseling, dates, etc. I stare in disbelief. These sorry social workers, who don't even know me are going to discuss, judge, and determine what happens with Ginger and me? I immediately flop to foul mood mode.

Kristi sees me reading the board and rolling my eyes as these people with less education and life experiences continue to filter in. They are here to discuss my life and that of my child? I suddenly am filled with disgust for the preceding.

Apparently being late is OK, as attorneys, therapists, and social workers arrive sporadically, like they're coming to a family picnic. Kristi and Cory know what I'm thinking, know what I want to say. They had warned me not to talk. I can offer no promises I laughingly told them.

I have friends who for years sought me out, seeking advice when hit with various problems. I have always been practical. I consciously weigh pros and cons of most decisions I make. Though I have made regrettable mistakes, I have for the most part made sound decisions. Those who know me realize that. But strangers in front of me now determine my short-term fate. They will choose the resources I need and mandate them, allowing me the opportunity to unite with my daughter. *Are you kidding me?* The sheer insanity of this process I sit in the middle of. When interacting with the characters in this nine-month nightmare, I probe to see if they believe what they are actually doing. The systematic policies followed by everyone, without regard to individual circumstance, are tearing innocent parents and families apart. Are they aware of this jilted process and its devastating effect on families? I believe they don't. I try to figure out for myself, do they think they are doing the right thing, or just collecting a paycheck? We all had a job doing that.

I pan the room dissecting each person. The social workers, four in all, sit together for apparent strength. Once THEY leave the security of this building they could pass as a whore, drug addict, or the same things they label us. And they are here to mandate me?

It's 8:15 and Nicole arrives. On time for her. She looks like a train wreck. But we all are. We're like prisoners in front of a parole board. We are parents condemned by the pretentious ones that surround us. I would love to run into or spend time with any of these people outside these concrete walls. I would love to debate any topic with any of them. But mainly, the topics everyone in this room appears to have trouble with; impartiality, respect, integrity, justice, truth, and objectivity. But the one item I would choose if just one were available is are you fair? At the end of your day, year or life, can you say I treated people with respect, dignity, and fairness? Or do you have guilt, hiding behind a badge or license wrapped around your neck? I skim the room and count those that hide behind the letter of the law. Are you one to give a homeless person a dollar while walking with friends and then walk right by when alone? And don't misconstrue treating people fairly with equally. If you do, without realizing it, you are biased, prejudiced, and judgmental.

Nicole stormed out of the room after two minutes of being questioned. I laughed inside, having watched this movie before. I wondered if just one person realized her volatility on full display. *What don't you people get?* Everyone appeared surprised but me. She was being asked about her insurance card and why she's not active in counseling. She was then asked about her phone and why nobody can get hold of her. She has used these two excuses for two years, avoiding drug treatment, therapy, and anything else she didn't want to do.

Cory, playing the ambassador role, softly says, "Let's take a short break," while looking at Moffit, Kristi, and me. Outside of the meeting room Cory looks at Moffit while Nicole is returning from the restroom. He says, "We don't have to continue this in there. We can go to your office or mine and discuss this ourselves."

It was the nearest I had been to Moffit, now standing next to her. I look at her then to Nicole, standing on her other side. Waiting for her to respond I'm thinking this bitch is weirder than I thought. She doesn't answer but instead moves her head slightly.

Is she nodding or shaking her head no? Speak. I look at Nicole thinking she might answer. She's silent as well. *What a tandem.* "Nicole, that's what we should do," I said.

She then looks at Moffit and Moffit to her. Cory, Kristi, and I look at each other.

Wowa

Without answering they answered. No private discussion with them. Kristi, Cory, and I head back to the meeting room. Cory whispers, "It's fucking Moffit causing every problem."

"She can't get laid," I said.

The only reason I cared to attend this meeting was for one reason. My little girl's birthday party. No matter what, I was going to have a party. It's all she has spoken of for the last month. The last three to four weeks I told Alex, Tylaiha, and Cory how important this was. Not to me but to Ginger. I was asked by Alex and Tylaiha; Where will it be? Who will supervise? And other petty questions. Everyone said the Family Meeting. We would talk about the party then.

With the return of us five and the meeting seemingly slowed, I wrote and showed Kristi on my legal pad, "Birthday party now?"

She nodded.

With a pause in the air I said, "I would like to bring up something very important. Ginger's birthday is in ten days, and she has to have a party."

Tylaihaa's supervisor, a lady named Shannon, wearing more make-up than a circus clown, spoke first. Trying to quickly think of reasons not to have a party, she starts, "Umm, well...where would it be?"

"My work (Western Motel). It's perfect," Nicole blurted.

"Uh-huh," Shannon muttered. "But who will supervise?" she asked.

"Stacey," I said.

Everyone looks at Stacey, and she nods yes.

"Well...ahh...yeah...um, would there be other kids there?" Shannon asks.

No, just stray animals

"Yes, and they could swim and have their own room to change and stuff," Nicole said.

"Okay," Shannon slowly says. Then in a gotcha moment she quickly says, "But will you and Gary be there at the same time?"

The implications were obvious. I may pick Nicole up, spin her over my head, and toss her face down onto the birthday cake. With Kristi's hand on my arm, implying "stay quiet," Nicole surprisingly says, "You know, it's important for Ginger to see us in a positive light."

I agreed, and added, "It is, it's very important."

Then, as if her rebuttal made sense, Shannon says, "Well, with the other kids there I really don't know.

WTF does that have to do with anything?

"It's something I will have to think about. Perhaps we could make it so Nicole is there half the time and Gary the other half."

I shake my head in disbelief.

Cory quietly leans over and says, "Quit shaking your head."

They're lucky it's all I'm doing

The meeting adjourns and Cory, Kristy, and I talk in the parking lot. On the other side of the lot talking, or plotting, are Nicole, Stacey, and Moffit. What should have been a meeting to unite, come together with a cohesive plan, is quickly turning into a battle between Nicole and me. The looming disposition hearing on the fourteenth is now bigger than before.

Kristi hands me some papers before I enter my car. Without looking at them I warmly thanked her and headed home.

What I'm fighting for.

CHAPTER Nineteen

How Does it Feel?

10/12/19

I'M WAITING FOR football to come on and decide to open the folder Kristi had given me. It contained the important case plan report. The case plan report is prepared by the case manager (Tylaiha) and given to the judge prior to the disposition hearing. It contains everything imaginable. It details what you have and have not done for three months. It ends with specific recommendations that the judge will rule on at the end of the hearing. I was now option A. I was now the recommended parent for Ginger to be placed with. The report chronicled for three months the dates Nicole had missed appointments for counseling, random drug tests, and even visits with Ginger. It read as though she was trying to miss them. The tone of the report had turned completely. Their patience with Nicole was gone. You would think I'd be pleased with the results. Being elevated to option A, lauded for compliance, continuing to do all I was asked. But I wasn't. It had a terrible effect on me. I was sad for Nicole. Sad for Ginger. This is not what I wanted. I had intervened for one reason: to be there in the event Nicole failed. Thank God I made that decision.

The case plan says it in black and white. It read, "Based on Nicole's progress a petition to terminate rights could be filed. If the permanency goal is changed and reunification with Gary is the goal, a petition to terminate is not needed in relation to Gary. This worker believes Gary will be able to assume custody of Ginger in a six-month time frame." I had to read this part over and over. I wonder if Nicole has read it. We had been texting back and forth, and she had made no mention of it. I did not want to bring it up, as I felt bad enough for her. But then the venomous texts came in. I had politely suggested she needed to be supportive of the recommendations regarding Ginger and me at the hearing. Her reply was "Fuck you, you ain't taking her with a whore living at your house."

I read the text in disbelief. I live alone. My girlfriend is not a whore. I have quit my job and devoted the last nine months and thousands of dollars to be there, rescue Gin in the event she couldn't. And this is the gratitude I receive. I try to reason. Fat chance. I ask directly if she's read the case plan. She wouldn't be responding as such if she had. No reply. I still don't bring it up. Her texts are all over the place. It's Saturday night, and I go to bed, but of course can't sleep. Nine months of sacrifice for Nicole and Ginger and she's fighting as though it's a custody battle. She caused this, I'm trying to fix it, and she's still fucking it up. I have rage and pity at the same time. The hearing is in thirty-six hours, and I haven't a clue which Nicole will be there. Could be the supportive one, the one that would agree and encourage Ginger's return to me. The one that would acknowledge "I can't at the moment, but thank God you can." Or it could be the Nicole that claims I beat her, there are drugs in my house, and I've got nothing but whores coming and going. Obviously I'm prepared for anything.

CHAPTER Twenty

The Day of Reckoning

10/14/19

I'M STILL TRYING to process what happened. Finally. Nine months to the day. At 10:00 I met Cory and Kristi in front of the Starbucks across from the courthouse. We were all upbeat, but Cory had a funeral to attend. He offered words of encouragement as Kristi and I head to the hearing.

As we chatted and waited outside room 210, the feeling I had was different. I had come full circle, in the eyes of these people, when actually I was no different. The only difference was I sucked up my pride and complied with their every whim.

I follow Kristi into the courtroom anxious about seeing Judge Whitt, the only person I've hated without seeing.

Time and time again Cory and Kristi offered their best legal advice. Remain unruffled. With that in mind I set my eyes for the first time on Judge Whitt, but he wasn't there. Instead stood a dark-haired gentleman in his late forties or early fifties greeting everyone as they entered. He informally asked who was coming while keeping an inquisitive eye on me.

I started to ask Kristi where Whitt was, but stopped. *That's Whitt you idiot* Expecting a white-haired sitting judge with bifocals, I instead see a coffee-drinking, standing judge as pleasant as morning tea. After all had been seated, he started with, according to Kristi, something very rare. I know it was directed to me as an apology. It's why I've been treated like Saddam Hussein.

He starts, "Normally I am off the record before we actually start, but I would like all of the following to be on the record."

The transcriber nods.

What's this about?

He began by giving the background on the case, as if he were reading this book. He stated this is a complex case, with more variables than most. He mentions Brielle, Tiffanie, and Ruth Harbour; the long latitude given Nicole by Jesse F. Stanford. He chronicled the start of DHS involvement, March, of 17' with Tiffanie, to the time Ginger was taken. He looked at me and said, "Throughout this time frame Mr. DeCarlo was no more than a shadowy figure." He stares for my reaction.

I nod slightly.

He continues, "Nobody knew who he was. But then, after establishing paternity, this shadowy figure slowly surfaced, and it is Mr. DeCarlo.

Thinks he's an author.

He wasn't done. He mentions he wasn't present at one hearing. He talks of Jennifer Russell representing me, without laughing, at another, and the last one when I foolishly represented myself. He's implying it's a perfect storm responsible for my nine-month fuck job.

Many things are running through my mind. Could be he is; sincere, covering his legal bases, Cory got in his head, or he's read the entire case reports. "I have read everything on this case," he coincidentally says, "so I am up to speed with everything."

OK. I turn to Kristi to see her reaction.

She smiles.

I'm trying to process his five-minute opening as Judge Whitt states, "Let's begin."

First up is the county attorney. *I remember this clown.* At the April hearing, the first one I attended begging for Gin's return, he asked me two questions as if this was a joke. The first, "If you were convicted of domestic assault and it carried a five-year no-contact, how would Nicole be able to see Ginger?"

I responded when I didn't know better with, "Well, we would have to get a third party to transport, I guess." This time he looks at me before starting and says, "The state goes along with all of the recommendations set forth by DHS, Your Honor"

What did he say? I couldn't believe it, as I sit up straighter in my chair.

Next was Nicole's attorney. Moffitt took the day off, as a different attorney from her office was there, sitting and talking to Nicole. She too stares at me before speaking, "We as well go along with the recommendations of DHS in the return of Ginger to Mr. DeCarlo."

I'm freaking out. A trick of some kind? What's the catch?

Next was Paul White, Ginger's attorney. He also serves as Gin's guardian ad litem. He is to advocate anything in Ginger's best interest. He is supposed to investigate, interview, and conduct overall background checks before recommending anything on Ginger's behalf. I wonder if the judge knows Paul and I have never spoken. Not once. His JOB is to interview me, come to my house, and look around. Talk, probe, and investigate. See what is in the best interest for Ginger. This man has not said one word to me. Ever. Not even "Hi," and I have sat NEXT to him at hearings. *That may be a small example of bad faith*

He begins, "Two weeks ago I had the chance to visit Ginger in Stacey's home. She looks very situated with where she's at. I would object to having her move again, Your Honor."

Kristi's staring at me staring at him. It's obvious why he's a public defender; he'd starve in the private sector. It is killing me looking at him and not being able to say a word.

Last to speak was Kristi, on my behalf. She was short and concise, telling the judge all I have done and implying there's not one reason, despite what Bozo just said, not to start transitioning right away.

Looking directly at me the judge then gives his ruling. "We will immediately start the transition of returning Ginger to her father. It will start with two overnight visits between now and the end of October. There will then be a minimum of two full weekends in November and the temporary visit after Thanksgiving. We will meet back here in two months to address how this transition is progressing."

The judge and I are staring at each other as he's finishing and I'm trying not to cry. The transcriber, directly between the judge and me, is also staring at me. Her look said, "Well, this is quite a change."

We wait for the actual papers, and I ask Kristi what the temporary visit means. She said it shouldn't really be called that, but it's the last item of business, before DHS would sign off on the case. I thanked and hugged her before departing to my car.

Tylaiha would have to specify the dates and sign off on everything in the court order. Knowing her, that would be an additional week or so.

I open my car and collapse in the seat, digesting what just happened. Nine months of hell exhaled out of me. I was emotionally spent ,and it still isn't over. The longer I sat there the more ambiguous I felt. I should be happy. I was, but my other half said, "Fuck these people. I was right all along!" I don't even know the effects this will have on my child. I thought of how I've been treated, disrespected every step of the way by people with biased, closed minds. I've been lied to over and over, made to do things Nicole wasn't even asked to do. Made to wait six weeks for a simple swab test, while holding Ginger captive, not allowing me to even talk to her. I thought of Jesse Stanford, the night she came to the house with two cops, the first meeting we had at DHS offices, and the power trip she played with me from beginning to end. I thought of the scribbled conditions she wrote on that legal pad, handing it to me as if saying, "Run away." Look what you people have done. My daughter is all I could think about. She needs to be compensated, and you characters need to be accountable. I'll confer with Cory when this is over. This is not vindication, because I didn't do anything. I had to defend myself for doing what? I want more then vindication. Vindication is when you did something wrong, allegedly. I want these unethical people exposed, and I want my little girl compensated. It's asking so much less than what we had to give.

10/1719

NICOLE AND I had been texting all week in preparation for Gin's party. It was now Thursday. I picked up the cake and headed to her work, the Best Western Motel and site of tomorrow's party. We spoke of DHS overstepping boundaries regarding us, Ginger's mental state, and how we are where we are. Hardly uplifting thoughts, when a festive party is looming.

Stacey, who had just gotten back from Las Vegas, finally answered her phone call from Nicole. We were trying to pinpoint the time for the party. She says we can't do the party tomorrow. "I have a concert to go to."

I then asked who was watching Gin while Stacey was gone. Nicole said Stacey's mother.

Nice. "There's not a fucking thing we can do about it," I said, so the party was scheduled for Saturday. We agreed to make it work.

The following day Nicole texts, asking if I've spoken to Gin (her birthday).

"No, but I was getting ready to call her," I said.

"Well, I just called and Stacey said they were busy." Nicole cried.

I immediately call Stacey. I asked if Ginger was there, she said yes, but was napping. I asked her to have Gin call when she wakes. She said she would. She never did. I tried a few more times with no answer. Likewise for Nicole. And I have to be civil at the party tomorrow. Try being nice to the person who denied you talking to your five-year-old on her birthday.

CHAPTER Twenty-One

This Could be Heaven or Hell

10/19/19

IT HAS DISASTER written all over it. My five-year-old's birthday party. And it's not for four hours. Stacey yesterday denied Nicole seeing Gin, denied me to talk to her on the phone. On her birthday. Everything I suspected about her is true. Playing God running amok. She's angry Gin is being removed. Especially to me. She hates my guts. *Woo-woo.* And now I have to go to the party and act civil toward her. Other than the time I arranged a meeting with Stacey and her then-boyfriend Dean, I have never really spoken to her. But the new court order changes everything. Her God-playing days are numbered.

I'm not supposed to be at the party while Nicole is there. And vice versa. She's working there today and has to be there, and Kelli says she's coming. She is not supposed to be there. Everyone (Stacey) will blame me. I have the most to lose. I have to be there for Gin and I will be. Kristi says I can lose everything gained so far, that Stacey wants me to misstep and then report it DHS, jeopardizing my over-nights next week. I'm supposed to be there half the time, Nicole half. I gotta be smooth, arrive a little late, leave a little early, and call that half. Let people see me doing that. This is supposed to be festive, but it's already tense. DHS again hurting Gin to the core. I want to ignore these factors and have a ball for Gin. And I may. Just deny everything if reported. That's what I'm leaning toward. I'm ready to shower, still weighing the pros and cons. It's what I do.

Stacey arrived with Gin and three other kids Gin's age, along with a ten- or eleven- month old. With her was a guy much younger, and I assumed it's her new dude. I wondered the manner in which Dean was discarded. The new guy, Todd I believe, had accompanied her to Vegas. I introduced myself as I mulled this family's dynamics unfolding in front of me. *Did they marry in Vegas? Who's this kid? A ten-month-old? How many are there? These kids live where Gin lives?* Trying to not figure this out yet, I head to the pool where the kids were swimming.

Overall the party was a success. It went as well as I had hoped. Stacey was cool, ignoring the fact Nicole and I were there at the same time. We even discussed how to answer DHS in the event they asked if we appeared there together. To top it off Kelli showed, out of thin air, nonetheless, at the very perfect time. Gin was opening her presents when she walked in. It was the first time since the tragic night Kelli had to hand Gin to authorities that they had seen each other. Nine long months. But Kelli had never left Gin's mind. She would bring over gifts and cards to my house that Gin would love to open during her visits. Gin got up from her chair and ran straight to her. While embracing they cried, as tears crept down my cheeks. Stacey, who earlier explained her dilemma about Kelli and DHS (DHS said Kelli is to not have contact with Ginger. Not because a background check showed convictions or allegations, but because they are DHS) watched the emotional connection between Kelli and Gin, quickly ignored DHS direction of the two. It was nice to see. I told Stacey during the party, the first real conversation we've had, that I would be hearing from Tylaiha next week regarding the specific days/nights Gin would be transitioning to my house. Before leaving I mentioned I would see her Monday morning. It was Gin's five-year-old physical checkup. I wanted to start being there, taking care of these types of appointments. Apparently I wasn't the only one hoping I would.

10/21/19

I ARRIVED AT Unity Point Pediatrician Clinic for Gin's 9:00 appointment a little early. After confirming at the front desk I was in the right place, I waited for Gin and Stacey to arrive. I wasn't expecting Stacey's entire daycare to come. I look up at the commotion from the front door and see an exasperated Todd holding one baby in a car seat, another by the hand, trying to open the door.

WTF

Gin sprints by them as Todd looks at me with "This is your fault" on his face.

I countered with a look of "You signed off on it."

Between the party and the doctor's office I'm identifying the reality of where Gin has been for nine months. The nurse calls Gin's name, and she and I follow to get her weighed and measured. Forty-six point four pounds on her three-foot, eight-inch frame. As we then enter the room, Stacey, holding a two- or three-year-old in one arm and yet to be completed forms in the other follows. Gin's expression, asked why is this kid here? I knew it was to help Todd's stress in the waiting room. Looking tall enough to talk, but wearing one of those one-piece sleeping outfits, the child looked anywhere from one to four years old. I stared in amazement as he emptied every drawer, like a crazed burglar, before the doctor arrived. I begin to feel empathy for Stacey and her new help in the waiting room, but the empathy filling my body for Gin, watching this loose cannon of a kid, overwhelmed everything else.

Gin's pediatrician arrives and was extremely nice. I'm barely listening, though. I'm thinking of my poor daughter, thrown into a bubbling daycare house, number of occupants unknown. I imagine fights, whining, and germs permeating the place. I become sadder with each passing thought. I don't blame Stacey, I like her, in fact, and know she likes Gin. All this does, however, is increase my resolve. The fact Ginger wanted to leave with me hurt once again, but I think I see it. I know I see the finish line for the very first time.

As we exit the examining room, my thoughts turn to Todd. I'm hoping he doesn't still have that look. But he did. And I don't blame him. Apparently instead of eight to five, he's chosen to help Stacey and their clan. It did appear Todd was watching one more kid when we left, then when we went in.

While driving home I'm trying to grasp what my poor daughter has been dealt. I now understand some of Gin's behaviors. I see the difference in her and where she's been for nine months. My mind thinks revenge. DHS revenge. The magnitude of what this has done to her I don't even know. I know the damage is more than anyone realizes. And it will be my job to fix it. A return to normalcy is my goal. Quiet, funny, and thoughtful talks. No fighting of time, other kids, and the rat race so many face. A time to secure, protect, and reassure. I hope we can rest, think, and regain our senses. I'm not worried about ABC's or numbers, because all I want is a giggling, carefree, creative, and secure five-year-old. If I have that, then I have it all.

10/22/19

I have been so patient. So very, very patient. But for eight days these vile thoughts alone, have permeated my skull;

Tylaiha, there's no hurry. Hey, no hurry at all. Take your sweet ass time, Tylaiha. This is bullshit. The judge issued an order almost ten days ago. Tell me when my little girl can spend the night. Give us dates, times, and a little bit of hope. You try doing this shit. My daughter's lived in a suitcase for nine months. The order says two nights from the fourteenth to the end of October. My attorney is waiting on you to review the order, which you got on the fourteenth, and to fucking sign off on it. Meanwhile my little girl just left from her visit. Crying again and wanting to stay. I'm ready to march down to that fucking office and see you now. It's shit like this that spells lawsuit.

I need to treat you pretentious power-laden clowns the way I've been treated, now reaching the ten-month mark. You weren't even at the hearing. The least you could do would be cognizant of the judge's ruling on your recommendations and then fucking act on them. Hello? Isn't that your job? But hey, I'm just some dude waiting to spend a little quality time with a five-year-old. ALONE. Take your fucking time. What's another week or two? Have a good rest of the week. Hopeful to talk to you, Monday?

10/25/19

MONDAY WAS A joke. Didn't really expect this. Neither my attorney nor I have heard from Tylaiha. My little girl is expecting me to call today, maybe spend the night, move to a new chapter. I am seething. This while I wait for Alex to get here and spend an hour and a half on a parenting course, Are you fucking kidding me?

Alex finally arrives, enters, and asks how I am.

"Not well at all," I said. I tell her how unhappy I am with Tylaiha, her complete laziness or sheer incompetence.

"Let me call her," she says.

"It can't hurt, but it's also Friday," I said. My experience was anything with Ty after Wednesday could wait until Monday.

Alex calls anyway. "Hi, Ty," she says. They start talking. "I was wondering about Gary's overnight visits," Alex says.

I can hear Ty on the other end. "I would have to review the court order," she responds.

I couldn't help myself. I tried and failed. "Oh no, she has the court order now," I injected to Alex, but for Ty to hear.

"I am sitting here with Gary now," Alex says.

You go, girl

"He says he's been waiting ten days,"

Most likely embarrassed caught sitting on her ass, Ty says, "How about tomorrow and Wednesday for the two October overnights?"

Alex looks to me, and I nod. Done deal. I waited eleven days for that?

CHAPTER Twenty-Two

My Biggest Accomplishment

10/26/19

I HAD ASKED Alex to tell Stacey, and then Gin, I was coming today. I was coming to her emotional rescue. I am your knight in shining armor. After nine and a half months I am able to drive over in my own car, scoop up my little girl, drive away at any speed, and take her any place I want. This was day one of transitioning Ginger from temporary foster care to my home, per Judge Whitt's October fourteenth, 2019 court ruling. I initially thought that gradual transitioning was a good idea. Until today. You zealots yank her out at the drop of hat and now take weeks to reunite her.

I figured Gin would have small sentiments of her stay at Stacey's. She did not want to leave my house. She did not want to go back. I was happy but stunned. I immediately think look what you people did. But what happened when I picked her up, for her first night back, tells everything needed about what this did to us.

I had arrived at the scheduled time, 1:00. I was to have Gin for twenty-four hours. I had never been to Stacey's. I knock softly on the door. A lady answers with a stare.

"Hi, is Ginger here? I'm Gary DeCarlo"

"No, she should be back in about twenty minutes," she says.

"I'll be back shortly," I replied. *This is where she's been?* I head to the nearest convenience store to kill a half hour. A doughnut and a cigarette, and I'm good to go. *I wonder if they told Gin I was coming* I head back to this house and quickly find out the answer. As I pull up I see Gin enter the house. I park and slowly walk back to the house. I wait and politely knock. The same lady answers, but Gin's in the background. Ginger sees me and shrieks, then runs toward me. She did not know it was an overnight. As we walk to my car she appears confused. She then stops, and with tears flowing says, "Daddy, do I get to spend the night?"

I engulf her in a bear hug with my tears flowing too and tell her, "Yes, sweetheart, just you and me." With neighbors watching I throw her in the car and jump in. We stared at each other still crying. Nine and a half months we waited for this. We continued to cry.

"No more visits," she shouts. I cry harder. So much trauma. "That's right, girl, it's almost over. I love you so much."

Cruising the way we used to.

"We can do what we want, go where we want?" she asks.

"Yes we can, baby; yes we can," I said. I wasn't expecting this. They had killed her. I was so happy and so sad. I fumbled with the seat belts trying to get the fuck out of there. Just my princess and me, flying down the road with windows down and music loud. Like we used to. I had explained these overnights were coming. But being told the same thing over and over, how could it register? I'm thinking so many things. This is the first time in nine and a half months we've been alone. The first time we've had privacy to say what we need and want to. It's also the first time in a long time I see her happy. And all we're doing is driving.

"No more visits," she abruptly yells.

Realizing they killed her as much as me, "No more visits" I yelled back.

"They were so stupid," she says, gaining confidence I'm bringing her back.

"I know, Ginny. How 'bout when they would follow us from room to room?" I'm trying to gain her trust, let her know I hear ya baby, and I'm so sorry. We're not even home yet, but I'm realizing what y'all did. You really did kidnap my girl. Put her in the deep freeze. As we parked I took a long deep breath. There is much to explain to her, and I want to be smart. I want us to be normal. As we get out of the car I can tell this has done more to her than I realized.

I had thought long and hard how we should spend these precious twenty-four hours. I wanted it to be many things, but with no overload. I wanted to convey so much and answer what's asked. I wanted to reassure, align wayward thoughts, and support this beautiful innocent girl all at the same time. Kelli had told me this was my biggest adult accomplishment, staying the course for all these months for Gin Rummy. I smiled and said, "Perhaps." But now I realize as Gin and I enter the house what really would be my biggest accomplishment. Erasing the emotional damage DHS has done to my daughter.

The bad faith and number of items I endured, all contributing to the damage done to Ginger are staggering. The hijacking and throwing her into a semi stranger's home, to start. The intentional keeping her from me, without speaking or seeing her for seventy days. Lying in court from Attorney Moffit; false reports from FSRP; no social history report for eight months; Ginger's guardian ad litem, Paul White, over one year's time, literally and not figuratively, never spoke one word to me. But recommended Gin stay in foster care; Tylaiha not responding or talking to me months at a time; being put in a cage at a hearing; Jesse's scribbled compliance conditions; Jenna, the therapist, misleading me on disclosure forms; being promised overnight visits four months ago, then rescinding them, for not one reason. This after I told Ginger about them. And being rejected for an additional one-hour a week visit, after complying for over seven months, with everything asked of me.

This was going to be calm and positive, a new start of sorts. We entered the house so very happy. Gin threw off her shoes, ran to the fridge, surveyed the inside, and dashed to her room. I wanted fun normalcy, if there is such a thing. We had to play games first, some unopened from her birthday. Perfect, I thought, as sitting together was always a chance for intimate talk. "Anything in particular you'd like to do?" I offered.

So sweet was she, smiling, she shook her head no.

This is ALL she wants Sounding serious I said, "We do have two places we have to go."

"Where's that?" she quizzed.

"You don't know?" I asked.

"No," she said.

"C'mon, man, the Theatrical Shop; Halloween's in three days." We jumped up and head to the car, but first figure out where to leave "her" dog, inside or out.

She's all smiles as she opens her passenger door, jumps onto the booster seat, and fastens her seat belt. I get in and fasten mine.

"Look, Dad," she says. With one finger she shows me how softly she can shut her door, something I told her perhaps a year ago. I can only look and admire what's next to me, more precious than life.

"Do you know what my new license plate says?" I asked her.

"Heck yeah," she answered.

"Close," I said. "My new one says GOTAROL. Now let's go." And just like we used to do, we were off and running.

We park on Fifth Street in Historical Valley Junction, across from the equally historic Theatrical Shop. Leaving without a costume from here is your fault alone. Gin remembered the place as we approached the front doors. She and I were here exactly a year ago, but this was much different. We were feeling the exact same thing. Freedom. Unabashed joy in being together, away from the last ten months. The owner sensed it, going out of his way this busy Saturday, to help my bubbling five year old.

Not knowing I would have bought her anything in the store, Gin settles on a pink Super Girl costume. We skip out the store and back to my car, when Gin says, "What's the second place we have to go?"

"God love ya, the grocery store," I said.

The first day and night Gin stayed was wonderful, but I wasn't expecting the torture she endured when returning to Stacey's the following day. I was mortified. I had suspected her spiritual demise was real, after seeing up close at the birthday party, and the doctor's visit, how the people she's been forced to live with are. Everything I hoped wasn't happening appeared to be happening. Not abuse or neglect, but everyday chaos and stress. The reality is I do know the last place she wanted to go was back there. As if my heart has not ached enough, returning her while crying left me numb and empty. All the preparation I did, the subtle talks and reminders that this is not permanent yet, did nothing. Letting her know how close we are could not trump what DHS has done. And as if my anger wasn't enough, Stacey, the uncertified foster parent and proprietor of the home Gin is stuck at, has started talking in extreme negatives about me. I decide to be the bigger one and address this at the appropriate time.

10/30/19

GIN'S SECOND OVERNIGHT was three days later, on Beggar's night. She was dropped off around 11:00 in the morning and would be picked up the following day. As usual she entered my house with smiles, love, and her magnetic charm. And all I'm thinking about is her mindset when she has to leave.

Nobody had mentioned a criteria for me, so I didn't ask—who could be around Gin and where I could take her. Not that I would adhere to any, but none were mentioned. Actually there was one. Nicole was to be nowhere around when Gin was here. A direct result of her lies that I abused her months ago. Still struggling with DHS demands and abuse allegations not ringing so true, it was as if DHS was punishing her. And that would be her perception and theme for months. I empathized but was also put through the hell she caused. I do not know until the state signs off on the case what is in store for Nicole. My hope is it's good for her and good for Gin. I will do what's right for everybody. I pray this ends in a good way.

Supergirl, Halloween 19'

Gin and I headed to Granger to see Kelli, Julie, and their parents, Donelle and Larry, the same place where she was handed over to authorities. There was no premonition or hint she had thought of that. She was just Ginger Rae as she rushed through the front door shouting, "Hi."

Letting her see and do things she loved and used to do was of course intentional. Implying this is what we did and what we will continue to do was my way to psychologically bring her back from the depths of hell.

With only three hours until 6:00, the city's starting time for Trick or Treaters, Gin asked repeatedly when to get dressed. Laughing, I said, "When the snow flurries and cold goes away."

It was freezing out, but she could not have cared less.

The following morning, when it was time to go, it happened

again. Gin begged to stay. I had warned her she had to return. None of it mattered. Pure agony again. I thought, *What goes on at Stacy's?* Something was happening I knew nothing about.

11/1/19

I KNEW NICOLE and Stacey had been fighting over everything regarding Ginger. *Great, this poor girl already traumatized now has to endure the remnants of these two battling* Nicole forwarded me texts Stacey had sent her. It was bashing Nicole's (and my) parenting, lack of discipline, feeding Ginger candy, criticizing Ginger's speech, etc. Those items were the theme over and over. I wanted to respond but didn't. So once again, as I have done over and over the last ten months, I ignored it. But then I get a text from Mother Teresa.

It had been a good day. There was communication between Kristi, Tyliaha, Alex, and me. We had scheduled the three remaining weekends until Thanksgiving for overnights with Gin. Wednesday and Thursdays will now be long unsupervised visits. And with Alex scheduled to come to my house Monday the fourth for more of my Safe Care parenting class, we could schedule the last item on the court order, the trial home visits.

I cringe as I see the text is from Stacey. I don't want to communicate with Stacey. It shouldn't be this way, but it is. I'm not going to engage in a battle with her. Kristi for one would go ballistic. It's what Stacey wants, Kristi told me. The end is near, the nightmare almost over. Continue as you have, I tell myself. Finish this job. But I seriously wonder if I can. This is my kid, and I'm on tilt. I set the phone back down to let it rest. I'll see you in a bit, I tell it.

11/3/19

I'M WANTING TO party. It's the best I've felt since the ordeal started. I reflect on the friction between Nicole and Stacey. *Keep your distance.* Kelli then calls and says Stacey just called HER.

"Why?" I inquired.

"To vent about Nicole and you," she said.

"Excuse me, let me call you back," I said. The phone had rested enough. I open the text from Stacey. To my amazement it read, "Pick up the next 3 Fridays not this week around 2:30 That is when she wakes up from nap. Nap time is from right after lunch which is usually noon here until she wakes up (which is usually 2:30 or 3ish)"

You make my kid take a three-hour nap every day?

"Could you make sure she gets a nap before she comes back on Sunday last time she was so tired and I couldn't keep her awake then she didn't want to go to bed. I need to be up at 5am on weekdays so I need kids on schedule. Bed time is at 830pm every night including weekends."

Yeah, because you get up at five o'clock you want my kid go to sleep at 8:30 on weekends at my house? OK

"I'll try to write out a schedule."

Yeaaah, I would like a copy of your schedule

"I'll try to write out a schedule to help her adjust there as well."

Yeaaah. Write me a schedule for me to use at my house.

"Consistence"

Yeaaah, you mean consistency?

"and schedules works best in all children of all ages"

Yeah, so does punctuation

"It will help transitioning go much easier as well and also with going back and forth."

Of course I had to read it a few times. I didn't know she was actually expecting a response, I thought it was just an illiterate rant. But she actually was expecting me to respond. A waste of my energy were my thoughts.

The next day she sends another text: "I'm trying to communicate here."

Any idea why you're failing?

"And no response from you."

Yeaah, I'll get right on that

11/4/19

IT'S 1:00 AS Alex knocks at the front door. GiGi's going nuts thinking Ginger is with her. It was the first time I was actually glad to see Alex. Every day after waking I head to my office, look at my calendar, and determine what tasks I have for the day. I had only one for this day, to have Alex facilitate the exact dates Ginger would be overnight at my house from now until the hearing on December 16. For Ginger's sake. I would highlight those days on my calendar and show Ginger just how often and how close we are to ending the nightmare. When she left after her last visit, sobbing in the car, she emphatically said when discussing her return, "I want to know the day," an unfathomable grasp of the situation for a girl who just turned five. After that day and comment, I pondered if there was not one positive thing that may result for Ginger as a result of her kidnapping. No. The closest thing I see is words mean little. For better or worse she will determine who she becomes close to, who she will trust, and who she will love.

With my meeting over and all Gin's overnights scheduled, I finally exhaled. Finally it was on paper. And highlighted. Three overnights a week starting immediately, Wednesday through Sunday the week of Thanksgiving, followed by three nights a week the first half of December. That would take us to the hearing date. If Judge Whitt signs off that day, it is over. If things run smoothly from now until then, it is over. But like Gin, I have also learned a lot. I have also learned words mean little. I have also learned who to trust and who to love.

CHAPTER Twenty-Three

My Refrigerator Talks

11/5/19

AS I'M WALKING aimlessly the aisles of Fareway, my favorite grocery store, all I'm thinking about is the last ten months. I know the toll it's taken on me and can only guess on Gin. I feel it physically, mentally, but mostly emotionally. I now have to change gears, change lifestyles. But more importantly I need to embrace those changes for the benefit of Ginger. I cannot feel exhausted, but relieved. I cannot feel anger, but joy. And I cannot feel entrapped, but peace and clarity. I have written and preached the importance of attitude. It is time I heed the words I speak.

I look in my cart and see juice boxes, macaroni and cheese, and tens of other items fit for a kid. No, I'm thinking, I need eggs, milk, beef, vegetables, and more of the basic food groups. Every thought seems to gravitate to Gin. In fact my therapist, Jordan, mentioned that in our session today. How impressed he is of the forethought I have regarding Gin. I have discussed potential problems that may arise. I have been proactive enrolling her in activities gymnastics and Head Start. I have discussed with him schedules, structure, therapy, self-worth, gratitude, visitation, friends, respect, chores, my book, and more topics that do or will surround Gin.

"One hundred forty dollars, please," the cashier says. I start laughing, as it's the most I have ever spent here, but when Gin arrives tomorrow I want the refrigerator to talk. I want it to say, "This is your home, honey! Take anything you want! Smile when you open me up!" I want my refrigerator to symbolize everything good. What's in here is clean, yummy, and here to make you feel good. It is fuel, energy, warmth, and security. When I speak of a good attitude, that is what I'm talking about.

11/6/19

I hadn't seen Gin for a week, a result of juggling and finalizing the new overnight schedule at my house. The two ninety-minute weekly visits were now one five-hour visit, the other an overnight. Every weekend with me as well, up to the next hearing on December 16. I was determined to have no glitches. We agreed on the 3:00 to 7:30 this Wednesday and Thursday. I arrive five minutes early and am greeted by the same staring person who answered the last time I was there. "Is Ginger here?" I asked, ignoring the lack of a hello.

Happy to see one another, Ginger and I ran to the car. I open her passenger door, and she climbs up and into her booster seat. We buckle in, and off to my house we went.

Entering my back porch we were greeted by three items: Gigi, a text from Alex, and a phone call from Ty.

They will not go away. I open the text and shake my head in disbelief. It read, "Hey Gary, Tylaiha just tried calling you but I wanted to let you know that Ginger does need to be in the back seat in a booster seat. Let me know if you have any questions. Stacey just notified me that she saw Ginger in the front seat."

Are you kidding me? So Stacey, who was nowhere to be found when I picked Ginger up thirty minutes ago, apparently was peeking out her window, assumed or lied, saying I had no booster seat, and immediately calls Alex as if her heart belongs to Ginger. That is what just happened? I search for other explanations. I stop, as there aren't any other explanations. But there is: she is just one resentful, twisted lady. I think of how to respond. I know how I want to, but can't. I will be tested to the very end. I had already looked up the statute regarding children and booster seats, as I became accustomed to dealing with these snakes. Ginger WAS in a booster seat. Ginger COULD be in the front seat. I text Alex back stating, "Iowa law mandates any child over 40lbs shall be secured in a booster seat facing forward. It allows children to be in the front seat providing the seat is all the way back."

She replies, "Your right but the back seat is the safest place."

I'm supposed to let it go, but I can't. I listen to Ty's voicemail. It says the same thing as Alex's text. I immediately call her but get her voicemail. I said I had a booster seat, someone was lying. Iowa law allows her up front. A lot of shit about nothing, I said.

Gin and I spent the hours hanging out. She had to be back at Stacey's at 7:30. I was already prepping her for the sad return. I highlighted my calendar showing her the increased visits and overnights. I had told her this is almost over. And I had pleaded, "I need you to be my big girl." We had made dinner together. Steak and eggs. Our pattern now was I cook the steak, she's in charge of the eggs. Neither of us cared that half the eggs went everywhere.

She's on her tablet as we start the long trek to Stacey's. I'm driving slowly, and she's being so good. It's 7:30 and we're five blocks away. I pull over to the side and stop, putting the car in park. She continues to play her tablet game and finally says, "What are you doing, Dad?"

"Sitting in the car with my girl," I softly said.

A smile hits her face as she finishes the game. My heart melts as she says, "You can go now, Dad."

It's now me wanting to cry. As we pull into the driveway I peek over at her. She is doing everything in her power not to cry. I ponder how many more times we can do this without fading. I wipe her cheeks and kiss her goodbye and tell her I'll see her tomorrow.

11/7/19

I ARRIVE AT Stacey's for our back-to-back five-hour visits. The set times are now 3:00 to 7:30, plus the entire weekends. I knock on the door ready to defend my booster seat rider, but I don't need to, as Gin answers the door saying, "You're late."

I look at the time, and it's 3:02. "God I love you; let's go." It was twenty degrees out, so I brought a new winter coat I'd bought her.

She loved it, put it on, and away we went. She is always as happy when picked up as she is sad when dropped off. Each visit is an emotional roller coaster, whether it's ninety minutes or the entire weekend. We were going to wash the car last night, but a new car wash by Stacey's had yet to open. "Let's go to the car wash" is the first thing she says.

"I'm up, but only if we can go out to eat afterwards," I said.

"Let's go to a restaurant," she implores.

"Absolutely." I said. But first were the five standard minutes of her questions regarding her visits. How long, what day, overnight, etc. I know how very important these questions are. I have even pulled over when driving to answer them, eye to eye, taking as much time as needed. I consider these questions her lifeline and information to provide her hope. They are at this time the most important questions in the world. With each passing visit and question session, I try to accomplish two things: let her know how close we are to getting this done and answer why and how this happened. I do know she has questions about the latter and deserves answers.

She has a good grasp of days, weekends, and what a week is, and I try to explain what's left along those lines. But there are harder questions that now come. "Why do I have to go back to Stacey's?" she asked tonight.

I knew that was coming, and this one required a pullover. "Do you know I don't want to take you to Stacey's?" I asked.

She nods yes.

"Do you know why I have to take you to Stacey's? That I would get in trouble if I didn't?"

She's looking at me and is thinking. I see her wondering what kind of trouble.

"But I am hoping that in three to four weeks I can keep you forever. Do you know what a lawyer or judge is?" I asked.

"No," she says.

"Those are people I have been meeting with for a long time. I don't work at Goodwill anymore because I spend so much time meeting with them. I meet with them to get you back home. And in a very short time they are going to let me bring you home. But I do this every day, fighting to get you back, and we are this close to winning. And I will not stop meeting with these people until you are home."

She is staring, listening to each and every word.

"You don't have to ask me anything right now, unless you want to, but I will answer any question you have anytime you want. And there is one more thing," I said. "Once you are home, I promise this will never, ever happen again."

We head to the car wash as I hope she knows what I said is true and not just words. If anyone needs more than words, it is now Ginger Rae. From the day she was taken, the only thing I thought of daily was what must she be thinking. I think of the exchange Alex and I had, when she referred to Gin as whiny. It caught me off guard. The second time she said it, I said, "You know what, Alex? Any four-year-old in the world who has endured what she has deserves to be a little fucking whiny. And the more I think about it, she's probably more mature than any other four-year-old around, so don't say that shit around me anymore."

Still driving I think of the day when I'm long gone, whether Gin will know I did all I could to have her back. I look in the rear-view mirror, and she's looking at me. We smile, and I think the answer is yes.

I park and we head to the deli inside Hy-Vee. What was I thinking? I had wanted buffet style, where Gin Rummy could walk along choosing her dishes. Well, it's the Hy-Vee deli, so chicken, mashed potatoes, and of course mac and cheese were her selections. It bombed, so we threw the majority of our food in the to-go container for GiGi and headed home.

On the way Gin says, "I'm making better choices next time."

I said, "It wasn't your fault. I picked a bad place. We'll go to a real restaurant next time."

11/10/19

WEEKEND NUMBER ONE done and in the books. When I took Gin to Stacey's front door, we rang the doorbell and waited. Gin looks at me and says in the way I have said so many times to her, "This almost over?"

"Yes, it is," I said, admiring her from above. So proud of this trooper.

She says, "How many more?" Meaning how many more times will I have to bring her back.

Don't make me cry little girl

She enters the door, and I head to the car as Stacey pulls up in a van, completely ignoring me or making any eye contact.

Grow up I shout her name.

She walks over as if doing me a favor.

"I'll be here tomorrow at three o'clock," I said.

"What?" she says, shaking her head.

"Did you get a copy of Alex's email and schedule?" I ask.

"I'm so pissed at those people; I don't get a thing from them," she said

"Would you like me to forward it?" I asked.

She's pissed at me, not them. She just can't formulate a reason why she hates me. "It's unbelievable, I don't hear a thing from anybody," she continues.

Is that a no?

She starts to walk away without finishing the conversation, so I get in my car and drive away.

I'm no more than five minutes away when Mother Teresa starts texting. And texting. Then texting. Did Gin nap?

I lie. I'm a terrible parent.

She's provided so much, I'm tearing it down, etc.

I showed remarkable restraint in not responding, which actually sent MT into a further fog, if that's possible.

Sone came over later that night, helped me snapshot the fictional tales, and I sent them to Kristi in an email. I apologized to Kristi about the length of time it may take to decipher each text. With hundreds of words and only one or two commas, it's not easy to read.

I woke up and texted Alex, asking if she had sent Stacey a copy of the visitation schedule.

She had. "Look at all I sent it to," she said.

I did, and the only email I didn't recognize started with Bambi@.

Bambi? She did get a copy So her rant when I dropped Gin off was made up. Like the lie about having no booster seat. Perhaps Mother Teresa doesn't have time to read her emails. But how could you, based on the bustle I saw there?

I also received Alex's monthly visitation report this morning for October. In it were random Stacey calls and complaints about Gin's behavior after visiting my house. That my visits somehow in ninety minutes transforms Gin into a human being. One with feelings and thoughts and things like preferences or having choices. Apparently these abstract things are not allowed in Stacey's house.

FSRP supervised my visits that Stacey complained about regarding how Gin realized there's more to life than naps. Their reports were glowing in my interactions and activities with Gin. Putting a shred of credence to Stacey's whining would be ludicrous. What is equally appalling, however, is Alex putting it in the report and not rebutting it. She authors the report and also supervises half the visits.

I kept my attorney up to speed with these Mother Teresa developments. They say Tylaiha needs to know now about Stacey's erratic behavior. I agree, as it will only get worse, potentially hindering Ginger's complete return December 16.

CHAPTER Twenty-Four

The Damage Is Done

11/12/19

WITH THE EXTENDED visits I'm becoming keenly aware of the damage that's been done to Gin. You can't tell a thing with a ninety-minute visit. The whole time is spent trying to play, love, and reconnect. A five-hour and overnight visit is another matter. Her emotions at times overwhelm, in a heartfelt way. She has in the last two visits come up to me maybe five times, starting to tell me something intimate, and then after pausing, says "Never mind." I let her know time and again she can tell me anything, that it's just her and me there. "Only good things will happen by telling me anything you want."

Of course she listens, but opening up may take time.

I now am 100 percent responsible for everything Gin. Her emotional, physical, and mental states. Her social skills, appearance, vocabulary, diet, structure, etc. But the first thing I try to convey is her ability to trust. It's been broken and has left her emotionally uncertain. At any costs I have to let her know I am her rock and will be here in any capacity at any time. That wouldn't be so hard, though, if she was here all the time. Telling her that and then dropping her off is misery. She's thinking and now asking "I'm already staying the night; why do I have to return?" As the days wind down to that December 16 hearing, the anxiousness she's exhibiting when returned to Stacey's is apparent.

I don't know the status of Gin and her mother. I don't know how often she actually sees her. I know no more than one or two ninety-minute sessions a week, at best. I have Gin call Nicole every time either has mentioned the other.

I saw Joe Nemmers, my second family therapist, at his office to-day. Joe is a super nice guy, and this was my second session with him. We ended up discussing two items after speaking with Cory on speaker: what we will present to the courts at the hearing and how I want to proceed with Nicole, regarding visitation and her involve-ment with Ginger. In summation I said I would determine and decide on my own, without interference from anybody or anything. We also thought trying to get Ginger, Nicole, and me together in a session may be beneficial to the three of us. But in short I'm thinking this is starting to waste my time. I'm ready to pull the plug. But after December 16.

11/14/19

IT'S THURSDAY AS I check my calendar: Alex at 12:30, followed by Jordan at 2:00. This shit is so old. Four weeks from Monday is the hearing, the hearing where everything could be finalized, the date I could pick Gin up, bring her home, and never take her back. I have to keep everything running smoothly. No missed appointments or hic-cups of any kind. Today is the ten-month mark. Ten months ago they stole my girl and turned my life upside down.

I have run through every hoop imaginable. I wonder how anyone with limited resources or a full-time job could do this. It's so criminal that it's mind boggling. I guess it's not criminal, as it's done every day and every hour across the country. I have wondered daily about two things when this is over. The publishing of this book and whether I have grounds to pursue a lawsuit. I will meet with Cory for advice on the latter when this over. I have written the pertinent happenings virtually every day as the events unfold, but there have been many things I have left out, intentionally or because the length of narration is at times overwhelming. In ten months I have read my writings from beginning to end perhaps three times. Each part is freshly written off the top of my head. When reading it I have I cried and laughed, but mostly become angry. It seems surreal at times. I had forgotten some of what I've written, read in disbelief at other sections, and wondered if I should change the perceived attacks on others. But I don't think I should. It is exactly what happened and how I felt.

An example of the aforementioned is Judge Whitt. Cory told me Tuesday he has cancer. He bent over backwards at the last hearing, apologizing to me, explaining on the record why I've been dismissed like a serial killer, but he was one who treated me like a serial killer, putting me in a cage out of the court room and cutting me off before I could finish one sentence.

I don't try to hurt anyone, and I do not lie, but when reading what I've written, I conclude there were ten months of too many things: malice, disrespect, bias, ill will, discrimination, and bad faith directed squarely at me. It is, I conclude, unforgivable. Unacceptable to me, my daughter, and all others who finds themselves in a similar predicament.

After Alex arrived and settled at my kitchen table, her first order of business was the misguided ramblings from Stacey. I had shown great restraint in not responding to her texts of "Me, me, me," and the less I replied, the more she responded. Nicole had shown Alex similar lamebrain texts she had forwarded to me. With Stacey's character surfacing the more she texted, Alex dismissed her complaints with a shake of her head. She went on to say Stacey had spoken to Tylaiha and said she was giving her ten-day notice on keeping Gin.

Alex was waiting to hear from Tylaiha and would forward that conversation to me. To have my daughter in a hostile environment from a non certified foster parent was both dangerous and insane.

11/18/19

GINGER'S AND MY second full weekend came and left quickly. It's a welcome change for both of us. We are growing together. It's surreal and emotional. I have asked myself over the last ten months what she must be thinking. This weekend offered some answers to this poignant question.

Despite Gin being sick Saturday night we still managed fun. I'm trying to balance several things as we start to settle in. I know we need structure, rules, and routines. Knowing what she's been through has made this part initially hard. This girl has been put on hold, treated not as a human but as a number. And that's as kind as I can be. She just turned five and is as bright as you or me. Nothing gets past her. She hears everything said and is perceptive beyond her years. I see her process information, formulate opinions, and store the information away. She has carried many thoughts, presumably bad ones, for the last ten months. She is guarded, resilient, emotional, caring, independent, and still grateful. I have looked for, but not yet seen, any resentment. She clamors for information, wants love and security, and craves meaningful relationships. She will love you only if she trusts you.

I picked Gin up for a five-hour visit, and Wednesday will start as overnights as well. I enrolled her in a gymnastics class called the Tumble Bugs. They meet once a week for an hour starting Wednesday. It is all five-year-old girls. We picked up her leotards this weekend. I am as excited as she is, but my reason is different. A return to normalcy from this misbegotten, interruption of her childhood.

It was only Kid Messenger, a place where Gin and I could communicate from different rooms in the house, but it was so much more. It told a story of what you people have done to her. It told a story of how she has felt then and now. And if you heard these audio messages, made by her and sent to me, you could hear what a broken heart sounds like.

Syncing our devices with Kid Messenger apps her on a tablet and on my phone, we discovered audio messages were easily sent. Perfect for a five-year-old who cannot spell to text. We at first sent one another silly-sounding audios. Gin sent many, from drawings to animal sounds. By night's end she had sent perhaps one hundred, most, of course, I hadn't opened. The next day with time on my hands I looked and opened several of her audios.

Most were heart wrenching but the most poignant one said, "Don't worry, Daddy; this will be over soon." She's telling me the same thing I told her every time I saw her for over ten months. This gift from God is consoling me.

CHAPTER Twenty-Five

Text You Very Much

11/21/19

DO THOSE THAT argue the longest or loudest normally win? Not in a civil world, a fair world. But if they're accustomed to getting their way, they continue that style of illiterate debate, as it's all that they may know. But eventually that classless, bullying rant is met with tempered logic and patience, with one overwhelming the other.

The bonehead texts flowed freely. Alex couldn't believe them, Ty couldn't believe them, but I completely enjoyed them. They were of course from Stacey. In short they chastised me for parking in front of her house, thereby hindering parental pickups of daycare children. I was told I was the rudest adult she had seen, after coming seven minutes early for Gin, thus disrupting her army of kids. There were similar texts, most making no sense, that I received almost daily. Alex said to me that if you had a child that she was watching, couldn't you pick them up whenever you wanted? My proud patience that I didn't know I had, had become pleasantly effective in ridding this nuisance from our lives.

On Wednesday night Alex dropped in to check Gin's status of an overnight. I showed her the texts. She said she'd be back tomorrow and we'd make a conference call to Tylaiha, the point of the call being the character of the person providing care to Gin. After the call Ty immediately drew up papers, and sent them to the attorneys and Judge Whitt, requesting Ginger be returned to me immediately. It took two days for the papers to be signed off on. Gin was now coming home with me full time!

That is not the end of it, however. The hearing December sixteenth, was a progress hearing. Though I had nothing to fear, I still trusted none of them. Yes, I wanted Gin and was ecstatic, but I also wanted this entire scenario out of family court. I have had one year of contempt for these people. I want them gone.

12/16/19

THE DECEMBER SIXTEENTH follow-up hearing regarding Ginger being transitioned to me was now very significant. With Stacey putting in her ten-day notice on November twenty-first, the way someone quits a job, it expedited Gin's return to me. It was my hope the travesty would be over this day. My goal was to walk away with Ginger and not ever see any of these people again. Wishful thinking. It was not Judge Whitt presiding but a judge sitting in for Whitt. The only negative came when Alex started talking about Gin having a difficult time transitioning. The only problems with Gin transitioning was when Alex showed up. It's called association.

As a result the judge ordered two additional months, twice a week, of random drop-ins from FSRP and Alex. Are you fucking kidding me? A blatant intrusion of privacy. Imagine someone stopping by your house at random, coming in, snooping around, and acting like they are there in the best interest of the child. They are looking for reasons to prolong this case. They can abruptly snatch your child in the middle of the night but take six months after reunification to get out of your life.

Cory just called congratulating me, not that this is over, but it's feeling that way. We touched on Paul White and his idiotic ramblings. If anyone would object it would be this imposter. We touched on how not to fall into any last traps. I told him Ty said anyone who interacts with Ginger needs to have a background check. He said that's not in a court order, and how in the hell would one do that?

Cory and I spoke about how all these entities now have to trust Gary DeCarlo, because there is not a thing you can do or say about him. We spoke of the finality of this, perhaps avoiding district court, and any further legal hassles, which brought us to Moffitt, Nicole's attorney. He wondered if the four of us could sit down and work out a visitation schedule. He then shook his head implying meeting with Moffitt is a waste of time. There was one thing I was thinking the whole time we spoke, but too afraid to ask. I wanted to know if this result would have happened without his help. What would have happened had I not stumbled into Cory McClure. But I may not ask. Perhaps it's an answer I don't want to know. Finally I said, "Cory I'm still writing and finishing that book."

He says, "Man, you should. I know an editor, and you have a story to tell."

"Thanks again, Cory," I said.

Preparing for Nerf battle in the basement.

CHAPTER Twenty-Six

Happy Anniversary, DHS

1/11/2020

IT HAS BEEN one year to the day my life was turned upside down. I remember every detail. Exactly one year to the day they invaded my home, stole my child, and violated every civil right I had and then preceded to scar my child emotionally. Why? Because Nicole wouldn't pee in a cup. Are you people out of your fucking minds? I thought imminent danger or neglect was the criteria for child removals. You assessed my household, concluded there was no danger or neglect, and then came and kidnapped my kid because of missed UA's? For one year? Who is responsible for this? The head of DHS? My case worker? Lawmakers? Do you know the effect this has had on my kid? Look what you did to me. I can only imagine the heartache you put on less-fortunate parents. How about single fathers? We know how much disrespect and unethical, unwritten shit you put me through. But I wouldn't quit. I told you from the start, each and every one that I'm not your typical client. But you tried to drag me through the mud like I was garbage.

How about the damage to my child you caused? I had glimpses of the effects on Gin when she wasn't here full time. I now have full custody and have her all of the time. The emotional damage you wreaked for not one fucking reason. Who's going to repair that damage? Probably me, the same person who had to quit his job to battle with you immunity-driven clowns.

Everything I suspected and hoped wasn't there is there. The fragility of Gin's emotional state. It is obvious with each passing day what they did to her. With each day and week I recognize quicker red flags, allowing me to redirect or stop a problem before it escalates.

I think of those seventy long days without a chance to even speak to her. The harm and insecurity it produced. There was no neglect or abuse of any kind. The assessments said that! They still yanked her out like a nugget of gold. Dissed me like I was Charles Manson. Made me wait six weeks for a DNA test result. Seventy days before talking or seeing her, eight months before filling out a social history report. Nine months before being allowed more than a ninety-minute visit. More items of bad faith, from every agency I encountered, over a ten-month time frame, than my attorney had ever seen in Family Court. This is what is going on in this country. Every day this happens to families over and over. Happy anniversary, DHS.

Stability is all I want. It's a daily roller coaster. I find myself going online and verifying the horrific effects of children taken from parents. Most studies are now stating the effects of removing children are more harmful than keeping them in the home, despite a small risk to children from abuse or neglect. Are you kidding me? I couldn't believe what I was reading. This can't be true. I would search another site. States it again. Child advocacy groups echoing the studies. These groups emphatically state support the family while keeping the kids in the home. Snatching them is a recipe for lifetime personality and behavioral disorders. Most information is on the effects of child removals. There is less information for parents once the child is reunited.

But this is what I signed up for, and I am all in. I am so in I have sought and scheduled therapy for Gin and me. We start in one to two weeks. I want to know specifically what they did and how to fix it. We are getting therapy for the trauma and anguish the state caused.

Part of the December sixteenth ruling reinforcing Ginger's return to me includes those weekly, random visits from FSRP and Alex. The biggest pain in the ass was still coming. Imagine just hanging out, watching TV in a relaxed mode, the doorbell rings, and GiGi starts barking wildly. And in comes Alex, "To observe." Then being asked, "What were the expectations you set prior to your last activity?"

What is wrong with you?

Ginger's mood turns sour because any presence from Alex in Gin's eyes can't be good. And Alex will report Gin is uncooperative, making my smooth transition with her appear rocky. This would play itself out two to three times a week. Alex shows, Gin rebels, and it's reported as incorrigible behavior. I tolerate this extreme invasion of privacy because the finish line's so close. The judge's order stated FSRP was to stop in twice a week for two months to check the transitional process. Evil-doers personified.

The first two weeks after the hearing, when Alex would stop by, Gin started doing things like hiding from her in a closet or under a couch, shit a two-year-old would do. Alex would look at me like this is how she behaves? Finally I would say, "You know what, Alex? She does this only when you show up. She is calm, caring, and polite for the most part. And as soon as you leave she will be that way again."

But none of this was good; it was actually the worst thing that could happen, because Ms. Goody Two-shoes, in her negative monthly reports, will report this behavior, making it appear there are serious problems in the household. The fact of the matter is Gin and I are finding a groove, our rapport evolving daily. Enjoying and growing together. Until the doorbell rings.

I thought hard how to solve this dilemma and came up with one answer. Make it a game with Ginger. I sat her down after deciding how to deal with this issue. "Gin, we have a problem," I started. "Well, we actually have two problems. One is Alex, and the other is you and your reaction to Alex. You cannot do this hiding, baby-acting stuff when she walks in the door. If you do, she will keep coming back."

She nods, implying she understands.

I emphasize the importance of it all.

In addition Alex was teaching modules of a parenting course called Safe Care, a basic guide for bumbling parents. She would come once a week for that. Topics were how to do items such as fix and eat dinner, play games, bathe, and put your child to bed, common logical items everyone should know.

I played college basketball and have a B.S. in physical education from the University of Iowa. I've been in the Des Moines Public School System for twenty plus years and have a lady telling me how to teach a kid to blow up a balloon.

For most of my life I have been a person who eats when I'm hungry and sleeps when I'm tired. I figured that barometer is better than a clock telling me what to do. I also know I'm not the most stringent parent when it comes to rules and structure. My child will know, however, right and wrong, manners and civility, and being accountable and responsible, so being told when, what, and where to eat; when and where to sleep by a person half my age in my house is nauseating at best. But I have come too far not to finish what I set out to do exactly one year ago. And I still was not going to say "I did it." Yet.

In these modules you do a practice one in order to advance or take the next one. I'm explaining to my five-year-old that we just have to complete them, tolerate the intrusion, and get them out of our life. She understands this pathetic logic. It's not the way we operate, but this is an exception. I would tell her what the topic would be prior to Alex arriving, and we would play the charade, and that included bedtime. Alex recommended bedtime be around 8:00 p.m. I didn't have the heart to tell her we don't get Gin's pajamas on till ten, but she sleeps every morning till 10:00 a.m., putting in a solid ten plus hours of sleep. She goes to school in the afternoon, so the schedule works for us. That's all there is to it. But not in their eyes. I had told Gin prior to the times, Alex wanted to observe sleep routines. When Alex would come, Gin would put on her pajamas and go to bed. Alex would leave, I would open Gin's door, and we would resume business as usual.

I thought since I wasn't the most interactive client they had, perhaps the worst, that I would try my best to accommodate. A few of these modules were activity oriented, and there are many activities to choose from at our house. We love games. Pool, board games, ping-pong, tents, forts, Lego tables, painting, mats for exercise, dance, and gymnastics, real musical instruments to play, and an amplifier with stand-up microphone for singing or to announce whatever comes in your head. You can hear the microphone throughout the house. There are many items you can announce. I do play-by-play of Gin's gymnastics, pool shooting, or racing around the pool table like a track meet. I can page her to come downstairs or announce it's dinnertime. My favorite is "Would Ginger Gist please report to concierge? Ginger Gist to concierge." A way to say, "Come here little girl. What ya doing?"

With the activity module coming, I told Gin after the activity to ask if Alex wanted to play some board games with you. Because Gin loves board game she also thought that was a great idea, but Alex didn't think so. Playing board games with Ginger is like going to work. It's just not that much fun. If you sit across from her, you're trapped. You can't win and can't leave. How much fun is that going to be? So Alex and Gin are playing, and I'm using the free time to do what Alex does. Sit and gawk. I finally get up and leave the room so Alex can really enjoy herself, when I hear Gin yell, "Dad, we have a problem down here."

Trying not to laugh I head back downstairs and said, "What's up?"

"Alex isn't playing by the rules," Gin says.

Alex starts to defend herself, but I interrupt. "She's not? Which rules are you playing by?" I asked.

"Montafee," Gin says.

"It's modified, and did you tell her?" I asked.

"No," Gin says.

"Well, you have to tell people they are your rules," I said before heading back upstairs.

The next time Alex arrived, Gin asked to play board games with her. Alex signed off on the activity module afterwards.

I have newfound respect for single mothers. Do I really? For mothers with two or three children, I do. For one child, it's actually fun being a stay-at-home dad, but it's very different for me. I'm retired. Virtually everything I do, is done on the slow side.

Kristi emailed stating we need to get ready for the next hearing, March twenty-second. I have begged her to get these people out of my life. Her solution is a bridge order, to have everything in order for the judge to sign off on. That would encompass having family therapy in order, a visitation schedule with Nicole, and her child support obligations set. It is, I hope, the last hearing. It is to see how things are progressing with Ginger and me. It has to be the last hearing. I can go no more.

1/16/20

AS I WAIT for Gin to wake up I realize it's exactly one month since the last hearing, meaning one more month of FSRP intrusions and two months until the March hearing. This morning Gin has an appointment with Julie Hewitt, her therapist. It will be the fourth time I've taken her there, and I realize since Gin has been going close to one year, I have not received one bit of feedback from anyone regarding her therapy. It's identical to every other entity in the case, Nobody knows anything, There is no communication between one agency and the next. I went to therapy every week for four months and nobody even knew it, including the case manager. That will change this morning. I emailed Julie two weeks ago stating I would love to talk outside the presence of Ginger, to find out things like her actual assessment, Ginger's mental health, any specific diagnosis, etc. Fundamental things you would think I'd be privy to. She did not reply.

It is ten degrees outside right now. Gin asked me yesterday when I was online what I was looking at. I was looking at homes in Tennessee, so tired of Iowa. I was already sick of this state before my daughter was kidnapped. Tired of winters and being indoors four out of every twelve months. Unless you enjoy cross-country skiing, I haven't a clue the appeal of this state. People talk of values and schools when speaking of the Midwest. Well, if your value system allows this state to operate with children the way it is set up, then I have a house to sell you. Throw in incredibly high property taxes, some of the highest in the country, and it makes leaving this cold-blooded state a no-brainer.

I answered Gin, "New houses where the weather is warm all year." We talked a bit of states that are cold, warm, etc. Later, after picking Gin up from school, the first thing she says is, "I told my teacher were moving."

"Slow down, Smokey," I told her.

I would want to see how Gin and Nicole's relationship progresses before I would consider moving. I wouldn't do that to either one of them. I think their lack of rapport is hindered because Nicole still doesn't have her own place. The basic foundation for growth of any kind is a place that's yours, that you can call home. Her visits, still two ninety-minute supervised ones per week, are still in place. She still misses some. And now, with a visitation scheduled being drafted, they are talking of continuing the supervised ones three more months, followed by a clean UA, then progressing to semi supervised. I don't agree with anything they do or have done. I should hand deliver a copy of this book, to all that aided or facilitated, in the most unjust year of my life. Once Family Court signs off on this case, my discretion regarding Gin is mine alone. If I decide Nicole may see Gin outside of her scheduled time, then that will be my decision. Fuck these people. I look forward to ridding these people from our lives by counting the days until the March 22 hearing.

I have told Nicole for months this is what I would do, let her see Gin at every opportunity, providing everyone is in safe mode. And I will. I want them to have a strong relationship. But ultimately it's Nicole's decision. I need to surround Gin with a strong support system. Between Nicole, Kelli, and Sone, three females who love Gin to death, that can happen. There cannot be jealousy or resentment from anyone.

DHS told me anyone who interacts with Gin must undergo a background check. Are you kidding me? Because Nicole has always run her mouth about Sone being in Gin's presence, saying Sone's a drug addict, she lives here, she's unfit, etc., I gave DHS Sone's info to run a check. And of course, much to Nicole's chagrin, it came back clean. Kelli is still on paper and DHS has always said Kelli was not to be around Gin, primarily because it appeared Kelli was hiding Gin from Jesse that cold, sad night one year ago. DHS has also told me my own children need to undergo background checks to interact, watch, or be around Gin. Kiss my apple tree.

January 20' Rounding into form.

1/19/20

IT'S FREEZING OUT, a Sunday morning, and Gin's sleeping in. I promised we would see *Doolittle* today, if she wants. I always need to find provocative things to do, as she's easily bored. Nicole texted this a.m., asked how Gin is. I told her she needs more interaction with you; you guys are slowly drifting apart. She didn't respond. Gin asked about her late last night, actually started crying for the first time she's been here, crying because she missed her mom. All I could tell her was, "You may talk to her or see her anytime," though Nicole has to be available.

I asked Nicole if she wanted to see Gin today after she texted. She didn't reply. So Gin will ask again about the movie and her mom when she wakes, because we spoke of both before she crashed. I will cover for Nicole, tell Gin she's probably working or sleeping. But with Gin, you can't fool her very often. With her two and two is always four.

It's the NFL Conference Football finals today. Something I rarely miss watching. It's action I love. Instead I'll be watching Robert Downey, Jr., talking with animals while I sit next to my five-year-old with a big tub of popcorn. It's part of the healing process.

Gin is exhibiting many emotional problems. It is so sad. She becomes unreasonable or emotional over the tiniest things, things that have no relevance, but they do to her. Everything must be done by her to her satisfaction. I'm dying to find the underlying reason. We are scheduled for child-parent psychotherapy on Thursday. I'm looking forward to it, but I'm sure it will be difficult to get her as enthused. I find if I'm not on my game, meaning a step ahead of her, she easily fades or falters. I find myself making sure I get up before her, to tidy and organize the day's activities. Without my doing so, she can easily get flustered and off to a bad day's start. Keeping her aware of why, what, and when events will happen is extremely important.

Her independent spirit is through the roof. I wonder and speak to her teacher about her habits at school. The teacher states all is positive, but I want to know whether she is social and friendly or introverted. Those behaviors reflect what's in her little head, versus whether she knows the sounds of letters.

1/21/20

A LONG BUT productive day started with a dental appointment for Gin. When the dental assistant came out to the waiting room and called Ginger's name, she jumped up and walked toward the assistant. By herself. She insisted she go alone. It's rather odd watching a five-year-old do that. I received stares from the others in the waiting room. One thing Ginger will be is driven and independent.

Today was my last session with Jordan. I had told Kristi and Alex I was through with therapy. Never needed a fucking session to begin with. Kristi asked if I had the discharge papers from Alex. DHS will need them for the March hearing, she told me, as well as the courts. So now I had to go into my session and convince Jordan I'm finished there, and by the way I need a discharge document. Trying to convince a therapist, who is linked to DHS, that you are finished with therapy is no easy task. Jordan and I reflected on the progress I made in the case from the time I first saw him. All the sessions focused squarely on Gin. The bullshit about domestic violence, the topic DHS loves to hold you hostage with, barely mentioned. My therapist knew it was bullshit. A woman can claim or fabricate abuse and you're required to take therapy? Fuck due process. I left the session having been discharged. Of all the superficial people, from every department I encountered, whose asses I had to kiss, Jordan is the only one with an ounce of integrity. The rest were puppets on a string doing anything they were told to keep their precious little jobs. A collection of unethical employees performing one of the most important jobs there is. That is one bad combination to be up against.

Thinking the case is almost over, imagine my surprise when I checked my voice mails. I had recognized the number from DHS. It was from a worker named Corene, who had been filling in for Tylaiha, who had been on medical leave for two months. She too had been to my home one month ago for a home visit. Home visits are not what they sound like. They are intended to give the employee freedom to snoop around your house without a warrant, under the guise of seeing how the child lives. You can imagine how they look around when unaccompanied. I know, because they were all on my security cameras. The voice mail said, "Gary, I need to schedule a home visit with you."

What the fuck for?

"I also ran a background check on your girlfriend and couldn't find anything. Lastly I need you to do a drug test."

I had to play the recording twice. Firstly, when running a background check, that is all you are doing. You punch in numbers and poof, up it comes. Implying you are "looking for things," conveys the background check is discretionary and subjective. Is it? Secondly, when requesting a urine sample, request a UA. Stating, "I need you to do a drug test," is both unprofessional, and reeks of bias.

Are you people out of your minds? One last shot to make me stumble. This is over the top. The request was truly a matter of principle. But wait, they don't have principles, so you're fucked again. I stared into space wondering how to handle this. What I wanted to do was refuse, but I can't.

1/29/20

I JUST RETURNED from pissing in a cup. Corene had called yesterday, her second call and request for a home visit and urine sample, or as she says, a drug test. The home visit is tomorrow. I can't wait for her to get here. I found out last night from Nicole that she was not contacted for a sample. It's unreal. I'm tested, and she's not? But Corene is new to the case, so she will discriminate against the male, just like every other one has. She will find out tomorrow what I think of the "random" drug test and everyone involved in the case, including her and her organization. I am quiet no longer. March 22nd cannot arrive quickly enough. I won; it's time y'all run away.

But the travesty of it all is that nobody wins. Some kids are saved by the system. We all applaud that, but why do we have to tolerate the overstepping of authority by workers and the destruction of so many innocent families? Most of these workers have immunity. Their accountability is zilch. They will do what the supervisors instruct them to do. It starts at the top, and from there it reaches upwards to the lawmakers.

I reflect every day, and still the last year is a blur. When I go back to read the insanity of the system we were caught in, it defies logic and belief. It is now more than two months since Gin has been with me day and night, and there is no denying they fucked her up.

Last Tuesday I went to our second child-parent psychotherapy session by myself. The first was Gin and me. The first few sessions will entail background information about Gin and me, the premise being our behaviors are shaped by our experiences, the hypothesis being how I was raised and my experiences will be handed down to my children. But I don't really believe that. I don't parent the way my parents did. I would like to think I took the positives from my happy middle-class upbringing and added positively to it, not just maintaining it. Some cycles of abuse from broken homes repeat themselves indefinitely. Children whose parents have substance-abuse issues will inevitably be predisposed to those same issues. In theory, that is. I understand the statistics but don't buy into the theory. So when the therapist starts fishing about my upbringing, I understand why.

The reason I am here is to find a way to understand and deal with any problems Ginger has, as a result of her illegal kidnapping. The trauma the state recklessly inflicted. They caused it, and I have to fix it? It's all part of the process, they will say. *Process* is a word included in many answers you will receive. It's what the agencies answer with. DHS, FSRP and the courts. They love saying the word *process*. It reduces their accountability, lets them ride the immunity horse. It's part of that process. You know, that process that lasts an average of a year and a half. It's where the state, in blatant disregard of parental and civil rights, invades your home, violating the Fourth Amendment, steals your kid, and then forces you to go to therapy and parenting classes, undergo mental and substance abuse evaluations, and much more, for month after month. And if you don't comply you don't get your kid back. You know, that process that protects our kids. It's the same one where they may come in the middle of the night to snatch your child. Without a warrant. That's the process I'm talking about. You may ask your case worker why you have to go to therapy when none was recommended, the case worker will say, "It's just part of the process."

You might even ask, "Why bother with the assessment?" But they will say that too is part of the...

I will try to get as much from the psychotherapy as we can, but it is hard, when all of the entities speak of trauma to children yanked from their homes, and mine was taken for neither neglect nor imminent danger. I can't get past it. I'm filled with resentment. Any of my close friends, who know the situation would understand my rage when seeing some of Gin's occasional, emotional fragility. This is what you people have done. And for what? Momma couldn't pee in a paper cup? How much manpower and tens of thousands taxpayer dollars have been wasted on this one-year-and-counting case? My dollar estimate when counting hearings, meetings, therapy, county attorneys, public and private counsel, judges, three DHS case managers, FSRP's almost daily involvement, and much more would be well over 200,000 dollars. That is for one case. Brilliant.

Twenty-Seven

Taking All I Can Get

2/5/20

WE STARTED OFF learning as we go. There's no handbook for a single sixty-one-year-old father and his five-year-old daughter. It's going on three months that I've had Gin full time. I tried to prepare myself in every possible way. I did not know how this would unfold. I did know I would be there 24/7. I am her salvation. I am also the one who she will exhibit her implosions and anger to. Our rapport is somewhere in the middle. I act much younger than my age; she acts much older. We speak more, joke more, and confront more like young teens than a senior and a yet-to-start kindergartner.

Gin is finding her niche, her sense of belonging. Both enhance her confidence and self-worth. She is also thriving in school. I am beyond elated that my daughter loves school. What any parent should do when their five-year-old loves school is take full advantage of such fortune. Do not take it for granted. Run with your enthusiasm alongside theirs. Continue to challenge and provoke them. Be involved and stay one step ahead of them.

Our Parent/Teacher conference is the 24th. I don't think a parent has looked forward to a preschool PT conference as much as I am. When I enrolled Gin, we were required to interview with the teacher prior to being admitted into the Head Start program. During that interview, with just the three of us in the classroom, Gin clung to me excessively. Knowing I had to tell the teacher some of the background of Gin, but hoping we wouldn't be rejected was a balancing act. The teacher, Crystal Woodward, has turned out to be one of the most positive people in Gin's life. She doesn't know it yet, but will at the conference the 24th. Gin loves school and her teacher. I am so grateful for both.

We got this.

2/7/20

I RECEIVED A letter in the mail today. A License Sanction Notification. It's when your child support is three months in arrears and they start the process to revoke or suspend your driver's license and any other state licenses you may hold. I didn't know I was so far behind. Oh, wait. I thought I had custody of my child. And where's my child support? When I saw the envelope I was thinking maybe they were telling me they located Nicole and support payments were forthcoming. What was I thinking? This is Iowa, and I have a penis.

I went back through my emails, and had asked my attorney December 9th, to address the support issue at our December 16th hearing. I also went down to the child support recovery office in December with my court orders granting me custody. The lady photocopied the papers and said it was taken care of. But she too is a state worker.

Because nothing has been done in District Court, I am still on the docket paying child support to the state. I am in arrears of three months. Juvenile or family court orders mean nothing. I finally reach a worker who tried helping me. She sent Suspend Child Support papers to Stacey and me, who is still on the docket to receive payments. We both have to sign the affidavits and turn them in. It's the only way to prevent payments from accruing, excluding District Court. However, I am on the hook for paying the three months that she has been with me. No one can make this up. I have tried not to contact my attorneys, as their invoices come like clockwork, and I suppose they should, but I've already paid just them more than ten thousand dollars. But money notwithstanding, it was a deal of a lifetime. I have more gratitude for what my attorneys did than I could ever put into words. I will be forever in their debt.

Today was the first day I have had contact with Stacey for some time, when she wanted Gin's Social Security number to claim her on her taxes. I didn't mind because she had Gin more than six months last year. I have asked Nicole for Gin's Social Security card several times over the last month, but she's holding the card hostage, the last bit of power she can hold against me. As if I can't get another. She knows Stacey wants to claim Gin and thinks I would give Stacey the number. I'm amused by the two still fighting like sisters home from school on a snow day. I had always thought Stacey's motives were money, and my premonitions were right all along. There are several items of Gin's still at Stacey's. Two weeks ago Nicole texted me and said Stacey sold on Facebook Marketplace a play piano Kelli had bought and took to Stacey's for Gin. It was the kind you step and dance on, like Tom Hanks in the movie *Big*. She had priced it at sixty dollars. Nicole and Kelli were angry about it, I was just amused.

Alex stopped by tonight. I told her about the child support letter. I implied just another problem for me to solve because of you boorish state workers. Her response, "Oh you don't want them to take your license. I would call or go down to the office."

Really. Ya think? Perhaps I was hoping to hear, "You know, Gary, it's one thing after another. Let me contact DHS, and we will get it taken care of."

That ain't happening. I replied to Alex, "Well, what the hell else would I do?"

2/11/20

THANKS FOR THE help, FSRP. The services you provide me are well, nonexistent. You are here to help and facilitate Ginger's welfare? I can't think of one thing you have provided for me. I have asked for Ginger's health and dental cards. I'm told that is in a different DHS division. I have asked for help getting my name on Ginger's birth certificate and am told by DHS it requires a court order. I take the court order to the state's Vital Records and am told the judge's order can't do it; I need a paternity affidavit signed by both parents. I give the affidavit to FSRP to give to Nicole whom they still supervise, and she tells FSRP she won't sign it. I should remind some that I do have custody of Ginger, and if we are still enduring the monitoring, please help and not hinder us. But the adversity I'm used to. Perhaps it's they who aren't used to this inexplicable union, of a sixty-one-year old father and his five-year old daughter.

This morning I received a voice mail from Child Support Recovery, and I'm thinking it's an apology, or maybe they have a support pay-ment for me. Yeah, that's really gonna happen. With each passing day I try to think of one positive thing DHS has done for Ginger and me.

I often think of other parents in the country, in a similar circum-stance. Those that weren't as lucky as I. Parents for whatever reason; a bump in the road or DHS playing God, that actually lost their chil-dren. My heart bleeds for them. This is so wrong and can happen to anyone. This must stop. I am going to find, through Ginger and my weekly Child Parent Psychotherapy, specifically what they have caused. They certainly know I am going nowhere. Actually I plan on going somewhere when this is over. To an attorney's office who specializes in lawsuits of entities who deliberately, through collective bad faith, destroy the lives of innocent, taxpaying, lawful citizens.

CHAPTER Twenty-Eight

Last Call

3/3/20

NOTHING IN THE last fourteen months has really been fair to Sone. She has taken a back seat to my roller coaster ride. Despite having spent the core of my emotions on the case, leaving little for our relationship, she had stood by me when others would have vanished. As odd as it sounds, Sone's relationship with Ginger grew without their having met. From the writings of this book and my preoccupation of Ginger, Sone could feel any new developments from afar. All that said, our relationship was far from solid. Bad timing, I would tell her, or perhaps we needed to meet under different circumstances. I would never have blamed her for running away, but she stuck it out, so meeting Ginger for the first time was a nervous time. It was also important I introduced them in the appropriate way. We decided she would stop by unannounced one day, like a friend stopping to say hello, and she did, but the familiarity of the house and GiGi didn't get by Gin. She knew immediately Sone wasn't a casual friend just stopping by. For whatever reason, they gravitated to one another right away. That in itself presented problems. Sone, fighting the delicate balance of "I'm not here to replace your mom but already love you to death," would follow Gin's leads in creating the boundaries between the two, but Gin was already all in, perhaps because she felt my fondness for Sone.

Throughout all of this I felt at times, as I did writing Time Capsule to Gin, I was too old for this. I know I am. All I wanted was to save my little girl, and give her a solid foundation to use, when I am gone. I now want to get to a place where I feel I've accomplished something, contributed a little, and gave more than I took. I feel blessed from here it was an enjoyable life and ride. I am grateful to have been a part, of many people's lives. My family and friends, I was quite lucky to have known. I felt I accomplished something large and real. I really did do the right thing, against huge evil odds. I stood up for what was right and fought what was wrong. I sacrificed much and put others before me. I think of Kelli stating this was my life's biggest accomplishment. I feel proud of what I did for Gin and those who love her. I felt relief, joy, and much resolve.

I sat in my living room looking out to the street reminiscing my life and those around me.

I see Sone pull up and park. I say hi as she enters the house. She doesn't say a word. An odd not-seen-before look covers her face.

Finally I said, "What's wrong?"

With a tear dropping from her cheek, but a smirk on a smug face, she says, "I'm pregnant."

Writing and reflecting in my office.

www.ingramcontent.com/pod-product-compliance
Lightning Source LLC
Chambersburg PA
CBHW072104080426
42733CB00010B/2202